A Wo

SELECTED POEMS, 1894–1921

Celebrated as a novelist and made famous by her novel *Anne of Green Gables* and its sequels, L.M. Montgomery (1874–1942) is far less known for also writing and publishing hundreds of poems over a period of half a century. Although this output included a chapbook and a full-length collection in which she presented herself primarily as a nature poet, most of her poems appeared in periodicals, including women's magazines, farm papers, faith-based periodicals, daily and weekly newspapers, and magazines for children. As a shrewd businesswoman, she learned to find the balance between literary quality and commercial saleability and continued to publish poetry even though it paid far less than short fiction.

A World of Songs: Selected Poems, 1894–1921, the second volume in The L.M. Montgomery Library, gathers a selection of fifty poems originally published across a twenty-five-year period. Benjamin Lefebvre organizes this work within the context of Montgomery's life and career, claiming her not only as a nature poet but also as the author of a wider range of "songs": of place, of memory, of lamentation, of war, of land and sea, of death, and of love. Many of these poems echo motifs that readers of Montgomery's novels will recognize, and many more explore surprising perspectives through the use of male speakers. These poems present today's readers with a new facet of the career of Canada's most enduringly popular author.

(THE L.M. MONTGOMERY LIBRARY)

BENJAMIN LEFEBVRE, editor of The L.M. Montgomery Library, is director of L.M. Montgomery Online. His publications include an edition of Montgomery's rediscovered final book, *The Blythes Are Quoted*, and the three-volume critical anthology *The L.M. Montgomery Reader*, which won the 2016 PROSE Award for Literature from the Association of American Publishers. He lives in Kitchener, Ontario.

THE L.M. MONTGOMERY LIBRARY
Edited by Benjamin Lefebvre

A Name for Herself: Selected Writings, 1891–1917
A World of Songs: Selected Poems, 1894–1921

L.M. MONTGOMERY

A World of Songs

SELECTED POEMS, 1894–1921

Edited by BENJAMIN LEFEBVRE

UNIVERSITY OF TORONTO PRESS
Toronto Buffalo London

© University of Toronto Press 2019
Toronto Buffalo London
www.utorontopress.com
Printed in Canada

ISBN 978-1-4875-0509-7 (cloth)   ISBN 978-1-4875-2369-5 (paper)

Printed on acid-free, 100% post-consumer recycled paper
with vegetable-based inks.

LIBRARY AND ARCHIVES CANADA CATALOGUING IN PUBLICATION

Montgomery, L.M. (Lucy Maud), 1874–1942
[Poems. Selections]
A world of songs : selected poems, 1894–1921 / L.M. Montgomery;
edited by Benjamin Lefebvre.

(The L.M. Montgomery library ; 2)

Includes bibliographical references and indexes.
ISBN 978-1-4875-0509-7 (cloth)   ISBN 978-1-4875-2369-5 (paper)

I. Lefebvre, Benjamin, 1977–, editor. II. Title.
III. Series: L.M. Montgomery Library; 2

PS8526.O55A6 2019   C811'.52   C2018-905058-6

University of Toronto Press acknowledges the financial assistance to
its publishing program of the Canada Council for the Arts and the
Ontario Arts Council, an agency of the Government of Ontario.

Contents

CONTENTS

CONTENTS

CONTENTS

Acknowledgments

This book owes debts to many people in the L.M. Montgomery community, especially the late Rea Wilmshurst (1941–1996), who tracked down the majority of Montgomery's periodical pieces for *Lucy Maud Montgomery: A Preliminary Bibliography* (1986), which she compiled in collaboration with Ruth Weber Russell and D.W. Russell and which remains a valuable resource; Donna J. Campbell, Carolyn Strom Collins, Joanne Lebold, and the late Christy Woster have all joined me in extending Rea's work using online search tools of the twenty-first century. My thanks also to Mark Thompson and his colleagues at University of Toronto Press as well as to Kelly Norah Drukker, Carole Gerson, Jacob Letkemann, Jennifer H. Litster, and three anonymous referees, all of whom were so generous with their engagement with this material as the manuscript took shape. I am grateful to staff at the interlibrary loan departments at a number of university libraries, including those at Guelph, Laurier, Prince Edward Island, Ryerson, Waterloo, and Winnipeg.

This book is dedicated to the loving memory of John Macneill (1930–2017), who, with his wife, Jennie Macneill, was a steward for many years of the Macneill Homestead in Cavendish, Prince Edward Island, where Montgomery was raised by her maternal grandparents and where she wrote many of the poems collected in this volume. His dedication to the land and his generosity and kindness to the Montgomery community will never be forgotten.

B.L.

A Note on the Author

L.M. Montgomery is now widely recognized as a major twentieth-century author, one whose bestselling books remain hugely popular and influential all over the world more than three-quarters of a century after her death. Born in Clifton (now New London), Prince Edward Island, in 1874, into a family whose ancestors had immigrated to Canada from Scotland and England, she was raised in nearby Cavendish by her maternal grandparents following the death of her mother and spent a year during her adolescence with her father and his new family in Saskatchewan. Raised in a household that distrusted novels but prized poetry and oral storytelling, she began to write during childhood, although few examples of her juvenilia survive. She received a teaching certificate from Prince of Wales College (Charlottetown) and, after one year of teaching school, took undergraduate courses in English literature for a year at Dalhousie University (Halifax), but she did not have the financial resources to complete her degree. During this time, she began publishing essays, short fiction, and poems in North American periodicals. In 1898, after two more years of teaching school, she returned to Cavendish to take care of her widowed grandmother and to write full-time, soon earning more from her pen than she had teaching school. With the exception of a nine-month stint on the staff of the *Halifax Daily Echo*, where her duties included writing a weekly column entitled "Around the Table," Montgomery remained in Cavendish until 1911, when the death of her grandmother freed her to marry a Presbyterian minister. After a honeymoon in England and Scotland, she and her husband moved to southern Ontario, where she divided her time between writing, motherhood, and the responsibilities that came with her position as a minister's wife.

Her first novel, *Anne of Green Gables* (1908), the benchmark against which her remaining body of work is measured, was followed by twenty-three additional books, including ten featuring Anne Shirley: *Anne of Avonlea* (1909), *Chronicles of Avonlea* (1912), *Anne of the Island* (1915), *Anne's House of Dreams* (1917), *Rainbow Valley* (1919), *Further Chronicles of Avonlea* (1920), *Rilla of Ingleside* (1921), *Anne of Windy Poplars* (1936), *Anne of Ingleside* (1939), and *The Blythes Are Quoted*, completed shortly before her death but not published in its entirety until 2009. During her distinguished career, she was made a Fellow of the British Royal Society of Arts, was named one of the twelve greatest women in Canada by the *Toronto Star*, and became an Officer of the Order of the British Empire. When she died in 1942, apparently by her own hand, her obituary in the *Globe and Mail* declared that her body of work "showed no lessening of that freshness and simplicity of style that characterized *Anne of Green Gables*." Since her death, several collections of her periodical pieces have been published, as have more than a dozen volumes of her journals, letters, essays, and scrapbooks. Ontario and Prince Edward Island are home to many tourist sites and archival collections devoted to her, and her books continue to be adapted for stage and screen.

Abbreviations

PUBLISHED WORK BY L.M. MONTGOMERY

AfGG
: *After Green Gables: L.M. Montgomery's Letters to Ephraim Weber, 1916–1941*

AHD
: *Anne's House of Dreams*

AIn
: *Anne of Ingleside*

AWP
: *Anne of Windy Poplars*

BQ
: *The Blythes Are Quoted*

CJLMM, 1
: *The Complete Journals of L.M. Montgomery: The PEI Years, 1889–1900*

CJLMM, 2
: *The Complete Journals of L.M. Montgomery: The PEI Years, 1901–1911*

EC
: *Emily Climbs*

ENM
: *Emily of New Moon*

EQ
: *Emily's Quest*

GGL
: *The Green Gables Letters from L.M. Montgomery to Ephraim Weber, 1905–1909*

LMMCJ, 1
: *L.M. Montgomery's Complete Journals: The Ontario Years, 1911–1917*

ABBREVIATIONS

LMMCJ, 2	*L.M. Montgomery's Complete Journals: The Ontario Years, 1918–1921*
MDMM	*My Dear Mr. M: Letters to G.B. MacMillan from L.M. Montgomery*
NH	*A Name for Herself: Selected Writings, 1891–1917*
RI	*Rilla of Ingleside*
SJLMM, 4	*The Selected Journals of L.M. Montgomery, Volume 4: 1929–1935*
TW	*A Tangled Web*

SECONDARY SOURCE

OED	*Oxford English Dictionary*

Preface

WHEN AN ADOLESCENT MAUD MONTGOMERY PUB-
lished her first poem, "On Cape Le Force," in the *Daily
Patriot* (Charlottetown) in November 1890, mere days before
her sixteenth birthday, her reaction on seeing her words and her
name in print for the first time was palpable: as she wrote in a
journal entry dated a week after the poem's publication, "I grew
dizzy – the letters danced before my eyes and I felt a curious
sensation of choking ... I can't find the words to express my
feelings."[1] Looking back at this moment in an essay published
in 1911, three years after her first novel, *Anne of Green Gables*
(1908), became a literary sensation, she called the experience of
seeing this poem in print "the first sweet bubble on the cup
of success," adding, "The first moment we see our first darling
brain-child in print is a very wonderful one!"[2] Yet, as evidence
of an evolution in her thinking once she had become a bestselling
novelist, it was the earliest experience of being *paid* for her work
that she later identified as the moment she had "arrived" – even
if her accounts differ of when that occurred.[3]

She was born Lucy Maud Montgomery on 30 November
1874, in Clifton (now New London), Prince Edward Island,
the only child of Hugh John Montgomery and Clara Woolner
Macneill, both of whom were from established Prince Edward
Island families with ancestral links to Scotland and England. In
the first known published account of her writing career, which
appeared in the *Boston Journal* five months after the publication
of *Anne of Green Gables*, she claimed, "Ever since I can remember I wrote stories and verse for my own amusement. When I

grew up I began to write them for other people's amusement."[4]
The publication of "On Cape Le Force" in 1890 was the first of
nearly five hundred poems published throughout her life (along
with an even greater number of short stories), most of them in
leading mainstream periodicals throughout North America. She
would downplay her periodical output in most of her retrospec-
tive accounts of her career, and even today, these pieces are rarely
discussed in scholarship and remain outshone by the continued
sales success of twenty-two books that she published between
1908 and 1939.

A World of Songs: Selected Poems, 1894–1921, the second
volume in The L.M. Montgomery Library, sets out to jumpstart
the conversation about Montgomery's poetry by offering her
worldwide readership in the twenty-first century a new sampling
of fifty poems, most of which have never before been collected
in book form. They were initially published across a period of
almost three decades, beginning in 1894, when Montgomery
was a student at Prince of Wales College in Charlottetown, and
1921, the year she published her First World War novel Rilla
of Ingleside. I offer this book as both the first step in a major
reconsideration of her poems and as a companion to her rediscovered final book, The Blythes Are Quoted (2009) – in which
Montgomery included the majority of her poems published from
1919 onward – out of my belief that scholarship on her work is
incomplete without wider access to the materials she published
in periodicals. In selecting and organizing the text of this volume,
I pay tribute to Montgomery's organizational structure in her
full-length collection, The Watchman and Other Poems (1916),
two sections of which are entitled "Songs of the Sea" and "Songs
of the Hill and Woods," but my selections go beyond the natural
world in order to showcase a wider range of "songs," including
songs of place, songs of memory, songs of lamentation, songs of
war, songs of land and sea, songs of death, and songs of love, as
well as a few additional poems that spill over those categories.
I also tended to privilege poems that reveal the ways in which
hope, love, and happiness intermingle (as they so often do in her
novels and journals) with despair, regret, grief, and pain. Because
I am also working on a scholarly edition of Montgomery's
collected poems, a project that will account for variants between

published and unpublished versions, this sampling is accompanied by brief notes at the end of the volume that identify sources for these poems and explain some of her word choices that were archaic even within her own lifetime. My afterword to this volume places Montgomery's poetry within her life, work, and legacy, particularly in light of the fact that she wrote poetry to express herself but published it as part of the living she earned as a professional author.

While I selected for this volume poems that stood well on their own merits, many of them are of particular interest because of the ways they anticipate motifs that would appear later in her book-length fiction. "The Gable Window," which features the phrase "a world of song" from which the title of this volume is drawn, focuses on the part of the house that acts both as a portal to the outside world and as a place of safety for the speaker, whereas "In Lovers' Lane" marks Montgomery's first attempt to memorialize in her published writing a stretch of land near her home in Cavendish that she referred to as "the dearest spot in the world to me,"[5] prior to her featuring places known as "Lover's Lane" (usually spelled in the singular form) in *Anne of Green Gables* and *The Blue Castle* (1926). Even "The Last Prayer," the earliest poem included in this volume, published two decades before the start of the First World War, is an early instance of a well-known pattern in her later fiction, specifically the juxtaposition, in *Rilla of Ingleside*, between the sacrifice of the soldier and the sacrifice of the mother waiting at home. Several poems anticipate the character of Walter Blythe, including "The Poet," which describes a male poet with "poignant vision" who is mocked for his gifts, whereas a quotation in *Rilla of Ingleside* of a line from one of Walter's poems – "A merry lilt o' moonlight for mermaiden revelry!"[6] – can be traced to Montgomery's 1909 poem "The Sea-Shell," a precursor to the way she would share her poems with Walter and Anne in *The Blythes Are Quoted*. Readers of *Anne of Ingleside* will recognize "An Old Man's Grave" as the poem Anne agrees reluctantly to write as an obituary for a man she barely knew – only to be irritated when his widow commissions an extra stanza from a talentless nephew. And in "What I Would Ask of Life," which closes this volume, the speaker addresses "life" directly, asking not for a lifetime free of worry, pain, or bitterness, but rather for the courage to accept whatever comes – a sentiment that would return in *Anne's House of Dreams* (1917), which mentions that Anne's engagement ring consists of a circlet of pearls instead of a diamond, in spite of the cultural association between pearls and tears. "Give me pearls for our troth ring, Gilbert," Anne declares, "and I'll willingly accept the sorrow of life with its joy."[7]

In "The Alpine Path: The Story of My Career," reflecting on her childhood experience reading the work of "Longfellow, Tennyson, Whittier, Scott, Byron, Milton, [and] Burns," Montgomery noted that "its music was woven into my growing soul and has echoed through it, consciously and subconsciously, ever since." Her own poetry, which she began writing in childhood and published through her entire adult life, thus grew out of this immersion into what she called "the music of the immortals."[8] But while her work was profoundly influenced by the poems of these British and American male writers, she adapted their music to create songs that reflected her worldview as a Canadian and as a woman, one whose novels have resonated with readers all over the world for more than a century.

BENJAMIN LEFEBVRE

NOTES

1 Montgomery, 7 December 1890, in *CJLMM*, 1: 53.

2 Montgomery, "How I Began to Write," 70; see also Montgomery, "Blank Verse?," 181; Montgomery, "An Autobiographical Sketch," 256.

3 Montgomery, "How I Began," 146; see also Montgomery, "An Autobiographical Sketch," 256. In all known versions of this account, Montgomery purchased bound volumes of poetry as a souvenir of this first experience as a paid writer. Although in these public accounts she identified her first payment for a poem or a short story, according to her journal, the volumes of poetry in question were paid for out of the prize money she won for a contest sponsored by the *Evening Mail* (Halifax) in early 1896; her winning entry, signed "Belinda Bluegrass," and her piece receiving

honourable mention, signed "Enid," appear in *A Name for Herself: Selected Writings, 1891–1917*. See *NH*, 44–46; Montgomery, 20 February 1896, in *CJLMM*, 1: 314; Lefebvre, in *NH*, 405n153. For some of Montgomery's comments about unpaid publications, see Montgomery, 14 March 1895, in *CJLMM*, 1: 262; Montgomery, 17 June 1895, in *CJLMM*, 1: 274.

4 "Author Tells How He Wrote His Story," 33.

5 Montgomery, 8 October 1899, in *CJLMM*, 1: 445.

6 *RI*, 42.

7 *AHD*, 27.

8 *NH*, 271. See also Montgomery, 3 March 1909, in *CJLMM*, 2: 216.

A World of Songs

SELECTED POEMS, 1894–1921

Overture

THE GABLE WINDOW

It opened on a world of wonder,
    When summer days were sweet and long,
A world of light, a world of splendor,
    A world of song.

'Twas there I passed my hours of dreaming,
    'Twas there I knelt at night to pray;
And, when the rose-lit dawn was streaming
    Across the day,

I bent from it to catch the glory
    Of all those radiant silver skies –
A resurrection allegory
    For human eyes!

The summer raindrops on it beating,
    The swallows clinging 'neath the eaves,
The wayward shadows by it fleeting,
    The whispering leaves;

The birds that passed in joyous vagrance,
    The echoes of the golden moon,
The drifting in of subtle fragrance
    The wind's low croon;

Held each a message and a token
    In every hour of day and night;
A meaning wordless and unspoken,
    Yet read aright.

I looked from it o'er bloomy meadows,
    Where idle breezes lost their way,

5

To solemn hills, whose purple shadows
  About them lay.

I saw the sunshine stream in splendor
  O'er heaven's utmost azure bars,
At eve the radiance, pure and tender,
  Of white-browed stars.

I carried there my childish sorrows,   *It was there*
  I wept my little griefs away;   *as a crutch to*
I pictured there my glad to-morrows   *lean on*
  In bright array.   *emotionally*

The airy dreams of child and maiden   *she was a*
  Hang round that gable window still, *child and*
As cling the vines, green and leaf-laden, *then grew up*
  About the sill.

And though I lean no longer from it,   *she has*
  To gaze with loving reverent eyes,   *moved or*
On clouds and amesthystine summit,   *house is gone maybe*
  And star-sown skies.

                    (window)
The lessons at its casement taught me, *The window showed*
  My life with rich fruition fill;   *the author meaning*
The rapture and the peace they brought me *and lessons*
  Are with me still!   *learned*
                                      from nature

(1897)

A lot of nature
  themes

Favorite word:

Amesthystine

→growing up but still
retaining memories that
shaped us

It was formative

→ representing something
  that's always there 6
through the years, it's the constant
↳sees it all

Prelude

THE POET'S THOUGHT

the power of sharing words & ideas (like a jewel)

It came to him in rainbow dreams,
(blend) Blent with the wisdom of the sages,
    Of spirit and of passion born;
(giving off light) In words as lucent as the morn
He prisoned it, and now it gleams,
    A jewel shining through the ages.

(1909)

The ideas for poems came in dreams

powerful & beautiful words

The poet showed the work to others

Now others can appreciate the work

I think this has some meaning to LM Montgomery's own life
↳ she wrote for herself but then soon started writing for other people to see

9

Songs of Place

I know a place for lagging feet
   Deep in the valley where the breeze
Makes melody in lichened boughs
   And murmurs low love-litanies.

There slender harebells nod and dream,
   And pale wild-roses offer up
The fragrance of their golden hearts
   As from some incense-brimmed cup.

It holds the sunshine sifted down
   Softly through many a beechen screen,
Save where by deeper woods embraced
   Cool shadows linger dim and green.

And there my love and I may walk
   And harken to the lapsing fall
Of unseen brooks, and tender winds,
   And wooing birds that sweetly call.

And every voice to her will say
   What I repeat in dear refrain,
And eyes will meet with seeking eyes
   And hands will clasp in Lovers' Lane.

Come, sweetheart, then, and we will stray
   Adown that valley, lingering long
Until the rose is wet with dew
   And robins come to even-song;

And woo each other, borrowing speech
    Of love from winds and brooks and birds
Until our sundered thoughts are one
    And hearts have no more need of words.

(1903)

We lingered there when twilight fell
   In purple gloom, and tender stars
   Looked out o'er sunset's glimmering bars,
And wood-winds wove their murmurous spell.

We stole that way when morning's gold
   Showered warm across the branches green,
   And threading sunlight crept between
The firs with glories manifold.

And at the hour when field and hill
   Were burning in the noontide glare
   We sought for shade and coolness there
Where wind-blown tassels had their will.

Oh, dear it was, that dim old lane,
   Its calm air sweet with breath of fir
   And echoing to the dreamful stir
Of soft wood-voices' low refrain.

Forever there was brooding rest
   In winding path and shadowy dell,
   A gracious benediction fell
To satisfy each varying guest.

The city's noise and strife were far,
   Ambition and unrest unknown,
   The joy of youth was all our own,
And through the dusk the dear home star.

Ah, often now we long in vain
    To steal away from toil and care,
    And, children-wise, to wander there
Adown the old, fir-shadowed lane.

(1904)

To-day I walked in dreamful mood adown
　　A garden old, where westering shadows lay
Athwart the tawny sward. The maple's crown
Was crimson, and the winding paths were brown,
　　And past me drifted on their airy way
　　　White fleets of thistledown.

There was a brooding and a mild content,
　　A gentle loneliness about the close;
The purple hazes of October blent
With rip'ning air, and branches downward bent
　　To touch my hair: but there was not a rose –
　　　The way I went.

The bleached vines clung where roses used to blow
　　In lilting June, and all the leaves were sere,
But sumacs tried to counterfeit their glow,
And pale-hued asters wavered to and fro,
　　The cherished darlings of the waning year,
　　　Reluctant still to go.

And, listening there, I heard all trem'lously
　　Footfalls of autumn passing on her way,
And in the mellow silence every tree
Whispered and crooned of hours that used to be,
　　And a lone wind like some lost thing astray
　　　Went moaning fitfully.

But not a note of laughter rang to-day
   In all the garden alleys still and sere,
There where our lingering footsteps used to stray,
And ever sought and found some dear delay,
   For those who laughed when roses crowned the year
     Were all now far away.

(1907)

THE OLD HOME CALLS

Come back to me, little dancing feet that roam the wide world
    o'er,
I long for the lilt of your flying steps in my silent rooms once
    more.
Come back to me, little voices gay with laughter and with song,
Come back, little hearts beating high with hopes, I have missed
    and mourned you long.

My roses bloom in my garden walks all sweet and wet with the
    dew,
My lights shine down on the long hill road the waning twilights
    through;
The swallows flutter about my eaves as in the years of old,
And close about me their steadfast arms the lisping pine-trees
    fold.

But I weary for you at morn and eve, O children of my love,
Come back to me from your pilgrim ways, from the seas and
    plains ye rove,
Come over the meadow and up the lane to my door set open
    wide,
And sit ye down where the red light shines from my welcoming
    fireside.

I keep for you all your childhood dreams, your gladness and
    delights,
The joy of days in the sun and rain, the sleep of care-free nights,
All the sweet faiths ye have lost and sought again shall be your
    own,
Darlings, come to my empty heart ... I am old and still and
    alone!

(1909)

THE EXILE

The roses are very fair that among you blossom –
   Nay, we have no such flowers ablow on our windy leas;
And the southern gale is sweet that barely ruffles
   The calm blue sheen of your sunny, smiling seas;
And your ways are warm and kindly – I would not ungrateful
     be,
But this land of yours, be it never so fair, cannot be home to me.

Ever my thoughts must be where my hungry heart is,
   Far away on shores that are very lone and gray,
Where the hoarse waves dash on rocks that are black and
     rugged,
   And the wild, red sunrise flares over misty headland and
     bay –
A harsh, bleak world to you of this golden shore;
But were I there again, I would roam from it nevermore.

Ah! If I could hear the wind in the glens of fir,
   The moan and murmur of pines that bend o'er the mountain
     linn!
Never is music so sweet in this land of exile,
   Sick unto death am I with longing for home and kin!
When shall I see again the land that bore my race?
When shall I look again with joy on my mother's face?

(1913)

THE SUMMONS

Today in the turbid city
   There came a call to me,
Like faint, unearthly music
   Wind-blown o'er a starlit sea;
I saw the sunrise uplands
   On the hills I used to roam,
And the old trees, green and faithful,
   That bend o'er my childhood's home.

Oh, 'tis long and long since I saw them –
   The still, untroubled ways,
The fields a-star with blossoms
   I loved in the olden days;
But the voices of joy and sorrow
   Are calling me back once more,
To the little house in the valley,
   That slopes to the orient shore.

Now will I hark to their pleading,
   Now will I rise and go
Back to those haunted meadows,
   Where winds of memory blow.
They call with luring cadence
   Above the din and jar –
I hear the homeland summons
   And I must follow far.

(1914)

Songs of Memory

THREE DAYS

Three days have I in my heart upsealed,
  One so bitter and two so sweet,
And even the bitter a joy can yield
  That makes my pulses beat.
Not for a lifetime of power and praise
  And every beautiful thing made glad,
Would I give the memory of those three days,
  Two joyous and one sad.

One, the day when I saw you first,
  Read in your eyes my sweetest doom,
And love in my soul that moment burst
  Like a splendid flower to bloom;
One the day when my heart had rung
  With the words that told me your love was mine,
And our eager lips had met and clung
  In a kiss that was half divine.

One, the day when we said farewell,
  Knowing it must not be otherwise,
And I saw the anguish you could not tell
  In the mirror of your eyes.
But saw there too that through the years
  Spirit to spirit would faithful be,
And that day baptized by your falling tears
  Is dearest of all to me.

(1901)

COMPANIONED

I walked to-day, but not alone,
    Adown a windy, sea-girt lea,
For memory, spendthrift of her charm,
    Peopled the silent lands for me.

The faces of old comradeship
    In golden youth were round my way,
And in the keening wind I heard
    The songs of many an orient day.

And to me called, from out the pines
    And woven grasses, voices dear,
As if from elfin lips should fall
    The mimicked tones of yesteryear.

Old laughter echoed o'er the leas,
    And love-lipped dreams the past had kept,
From wayside blooms like honeyed bees
    To company my wanderings crept.

And so I walked, but not alone,
    Right glad companionship had I
On that gray meadow waste between
    Dim-litten sea and winnowed sky.

(1910)

DO YOU REMEMBER?

Do you remember that lone, ancient shore
   Whose irised waters, stretching towards the west,
Into uncharted realms of sunset bore
   Our vision and our quest?
We stood together ... over land and sky
   A silence like a benediction fell,
   But the sea wove its immemorial spell
And would not cease to sigh.
A gray ship went adown the dusky east,
   Drifting in phantom fashion past our ken,
And a white gull soared where the heaven was fleeced
   To wide, free wastes again.
With lifted eyes we watched its glorious flight,
   And saw a sinking moon beyond the bar,
   A silver shallop moored unto a star
In haven of the night.
Behind us was a land all dim with pines
   Garmented in the twilight; and before
Lay the dark ocean symbolled with the signs
   Of untranslated lore;
And we, drawn nearer, felt our hearts beset
   With love that needed not of words to be
   Best understood ... Oh, time stands still for me
And holds that moment yet!

(1911)

A wide spring meadow in a rosy dawn
    Bedropt with virgin buds; an orient sky
Fleeced with a dappled cloud but half withdrawn;
    A mad wind blowing by,
O'er slopes of rippling grass and glens apart;
    A brackened path to a wild woodland place;
    A limpid pool with a fair, laughing face
Mirrored within its heart.

An ancient garden brimmed with summer sun
    Upon a still and slumberous afternoon;
Old walks and pleasaunces with shadows spun
    Where honeyed odours swoon;
A velvet turf with blossoms garlanded;
    A hedge of Mary-lilies white and tall;
    And, shining out against a lichened wall,
A stately golden head.

An autumn hilltop in the sunset hue;
    Pine boughs uptossed against the crystal west;
And girdled with the twilight dim and blue,
    A valley peace-possessed;
A high-sprung heaven stained with colours rare,
    A sheen of moonrise on the sea afar,
    And, bright and soft as any glimmering star,
Eyes holy as a prayer.

(1912)

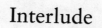

Interlude

THE SINGER

A song, a song of courage, of fellowship and cheer,
    That weary hearts may echo and lonely hearts may hear.
A song, oh, sing it bravely, with tenderness and truth,
    For every age a message, gray years and golden youth.

A song of hope undaunted, of faith in God and man,
    For all of fine and noble that lights our earthly span;
A song of human sorrow alight with human love,
    A song of high endeavor that coming days may prove!

Sing thus, oh faithful singer, and those who hear your song
    Will echo it with gladness, the whole wide world along.
Till all who wage a contest with foes of doubt and care
    Will catch your notes of promise and sing them everywhere!

(1906)

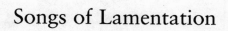

Songs of Lamentation

IRREVOCABLE

Once on a time I spoke a word
That was bitter of meaning and harsh of tone,
And it went as straight as a poisoned dart
To the very core of a true friend's heart,
And the beautiful page of our love was blurred
Forevermore by that word alone.

Once on a time I cast a sneer
At the small mistake of one I knew,
And his soul, discouraged, let slip the rope
That anchored it to the shore of hope,
And drifted out on a sea of fear,
To waves of failure and winds untrue.

Once on a time I whispered a tale
Tainted with malice, and far and near
It flew, to cast on a spotless name
The upas shade of a hinted shame,
And wherever it reached it left a trail
Across the promise of many a year.

Never that word could be unsaid
That lost me a friendship old and true –
Never that sneer might be undone
That broke the trust of an erring one –
Never untold the tale that sped
To blight and baffle a lifetime through.

(1898)

I would be well if once again I saw the dancing shadows
    Skim o'er the daisied grasses 'neath the breezes' flying feet,
If once again I lingered in the green, rain-freshened meadows,
    And heard the wilding thrushes sing in many a dear retreat.

If I could feel the woodland winds in silent byways blowing,
    And hear the green leaves rustling at my casement in the
        night,
If I could see the dawnlight o'er the hills of sunrise glowing,
    And drink with thirsty eagerness the breath of orchards
        white,

Oh, then I know this weary pain would leave me and forever,
    And health would come again to me with every spring-time
        breath;
I would go forth with gladdened eyes and joyful heart, and
        never
    Would there be lonely fields and snows to make me think of
    death.

If I could roam in mellow days where blithe wild roses blossom,
    And loiter in the field-paths that my feet have trod of yore,
If I could lay my fevered cheek close to the dear earth's bosom,
    And feel her deep, life-giving peace fill all my heart once
    more!

Oh, will the winter never pass to greet the spring's returning?
    How long the days are seeming and my endless nights of
        pain,
While deep within my restless heart still throbs this ceaseless
        yearning
    For one dear glimpse of summer woods and summer fields
    again.

Then, when the mornings break aglow o'er hills untouched by
    shadows,
  And gem-like dewdrops glisten in each chaliced lily-bell,
When the smile of spring has wakened into life the raptured
    meadows,
  Then new life will stir within me and I know I shall be well.

(1900)

Oh, darkness and silence hold their sway
    At the midnight's solemn hour,
And the dreams of many a yesterday
    Return with a fleeting power
                        Once more
To thrill the heart they stirred of yore.

Griefs that cost us many a sigh,
    Fancies long a-cold,
Dreams that seemed too bright to die,
    And pangs that we felt of old
                        All come
Like spectral shadows thro' the gloom.

Passions that burned in the vanished years
    With a life so strong and deep,
Return to haunt in their phantom guise
    The pillow that knows not sleep,
                        When low
The waves of night seem to ebb and flow.

All the mistakes that marred our life,
    All we have failed to do,
Shattered ambition and fruitless strife,
    So much, so much to rue!
                        Ah me,
But the night has a grewsome sorcery!

Happiness that our hearts have missed
   Still aches like the ghost of pain;
Longed-for lips that we never kissed
   Mock us with smiles again.
                 The heart
Looks on its dead ere the stars depart.

Oh, what a fearful and mystic power
   Have the watches of the night!
The wealth of the bygone is their dower,
   And ghosts of a dead delight
                 To and fro
Thro' the gates of darkness come and go.

(1900)

If I had known how much of lasting good
  One little word breathed in all tenderness
Would garner in – if I had understood
  How much it meant to a soul faint with stress,
I would have spoken it with gladness great,
Nor learned the rueful meaning of too late.

If I had known how deep for harm and ill
  One little poisoned, laughing sneer would sting
Into another's heart, there to distil
  Its bitterest venom like a viperous thing,
I never would have spoken in such tone
  Such cruel, careless words – if I had known!

(1903)

THE BOOK

I wrote therein the bitterness
    That grief into my life had brought,
The anguish of the lonely night,
    The pain each troubled day had wrought.

And when my sorrow thus was writ,
    I called my book "the song of tears";
But, reading, lo! I found it held
    The wisdom of unnumbered years!

(1906)

If I could see you once, but once, as in
   The days of yore, how would my heart rejoice!
   Could I but hear again your tender voice,
And catch the glory of the soul within
Your eyes inspired, I think that I could win
   All my heart longs for in the race of life!
   I should be fitly guerdoned for the strife,
And all my being seem once more akin
To God and good ... If I once more might look
   Upon your strong, pure face and gather there,
As from the pages of some holy book,
   Courage and faith to conquer and to dare
All things of evil, whatsoe'er they be –
This were the boon that you would bring to me.

If I might see you once! The thought is vain
   And full of bitterness, for those clear eyes
   Have looked upon the light of Paradise
And turn not back to our dim star again.
But yet, dear heart, I kiss the lips of pain,
   And teach my soul to hold your standard true,
   And live each passing moment as if you
Were by me still to comfort and sustain,
That so, when we shall meet, I may not shrink
   Before your eyes or fear myself so base
That you, pure, stainless spirit, would not think
   Me worthy thus to gaze upon your face.
And so, through sorrow, you must ever be
An inspiration and a guide to me.

(1907)

THE MOTHER

Here I lean over you, small son, sleeping
Warm in my arms,
And I con to my heart all your dew-fresh charms,
As you lie close, close in my hungry hold ...
Your hair like a miser's dream of gold,
And the white rose of your face far fairer,
Finer, and rarer
Than all the flowers in the young year's keeping;
Over lips half parted your low breath creeping
Is sweeter than violets in April grasses;
Though your eyes are fast shut I can see their blue,
Splendid and soft as starshine in heaven,
With all the joyance and wisdom given
From the many souls who have stanchly striven
Through the dead years to be strong and true.

Those fine little feet in my worn hands holden ...
Where will they tread?
Valleys of shadow or heights dawn-red?
And those silken fingers, O, wee, white son,
What valorous deeds shall by them be done
In the future that yet so distant is seeming
To my fond dreaming?
What words all so musical and golden
With starry truth and poesy olden
Shall those lips speak in the years on-coming?
O, child of mine, with waxen brow,
Surely your words of that dim to-morrow
Rapture and power and grace must borrow
From the poignant love and holy sorrow
Of the heart that shrines and cradles you now!

Some bitter day you will love another,
To her will bear
Love-gifts and woo her ... then must I share
You and your tenderness! Now you are mine
From your feet to your hair so golden and fine,
And your crumpled finger-tips ... mine completely,
Wholly and sweetly;
Mine with kisses deep to smother,
No one so near to you now as your mother!
Others may hear your words of beauty,
But your precious silence is mine alone;
Here in my arms I have enrolled you,
Away from the grasping world I fold you,
Flesh of my flesh and bone of my bone!

(1916)

Songs of War

THE LAST PRAYER

A young soldier was found mortally wounded on the field after a hard-fought battle. As they bent over him he opened his eyes, and murmuring "now I lay me down to sleep," died.

The carnage of the battle day was done;
Behind the red hills sank the shamed sun;
And shuddering nature drew across her sight,
Shrinking and sad, the mantle of the night.
All seemed at rest when from the twilight skies
The stars looked down like pitying angels' eyes
On that dread field, which, since the Dawn's first ray
Had purpled o'er the cheek of pallid Day,
Had echoed to the battle thunder's roll –
The mighty dirge of many a brave man's soul.
And one was there who, mid the smoke and flame
Of Death's wild havoc, bore a soldier's name.
A mere youth still, who, on that alien strand
Had fought the battles of his native land
Bravely and well; the slender boyish form
Was ever in the thickest battle storm;
His was the dauntless spirit all to dare,
Duty or danger called – and he was there.
But Death's fell minion well fulfilled its part,
And sheathed itself too near that brave young heart.
And far from Albion's wave-encircled shore,
Her soldier-hero fell, to rise no more.
There, too, his comrades, at the close of day
Found him as in his own life's-blood he lay.
Over his pallid brow, where one might trace
Some lingering remnant of its childhood grace,
The death damp fell; but, even as they said
With tender, reverend, sadness "He is dead,"
His dark eyes opened; thro' the shades of night

They seemed to pierce with strange unearthly light.
Where looked those bright eyes? Far beyond the stars,
Where Heaven sets its utmost purple bars?
Or did they seek, across the restless sea,
A spot, where daisies starred an English lea?
Where, in the sunshine of her cottage door,
Whose porch would echo to his step no more,
His aged mother sat, her gentle eyes
Bright with reflected light from Paradise;
Lovingly thinking of her wandering boy,
Her widow's comfort, and her mother's joy.
Saw he himself again, life but begun,
Kneeling, hands clasped, by her at set of sun,
While dimly conscious of some angel near,
He lisped the little prayer to childhood dear?
Perchance he felt her toil-worn hand once more,
In tender benediction, as of yore,
Rest its light touch upon his curly head,
And her dear kiss, when the "good night" was said.
His pale lips move, as Death's dark shadows creep,
And softly murmur, "Lay me down to sleep,"
A shuddering breath, a sigh – his spirit fled
To that far land where pain and grief are dead,
Where glory sleeps upon a tideless shore,
And Earth's dark vapours dim our eyes no more.

(1894)

The poet sang of a battle-field
   Where doughty deeds were done,
Where stout blows rang on helm and shield
   And a kingdom's fate was spun
With the scarlet thread of victory,
And honor from death's grim revelry
   Like a flame-red flower was won!
So bravely he sang that all who heard
With the sting of the fight and triumph were stirred,
And they cried, "Let us blazon his name on high,
He has sung a song that will never die!"

Again, full-throated, he sang of fame
   And ambition's honeyed lure,
Of the chaplet that garlands a mighty name,
Till his listeners fired with the god-like flame
   To do, to dare, to endure!
The thirsty lips of the world were fain
The cup of glamor he vaunted to drain.
And the people murmured as he went by,
"He has sung a song that will never die!"

And once more he sang, all low and apart,
A song of the love that was born in his heart,
Thinking to voice in unfettered strain
Its sweet delight and its sweeter pain;
Nothing he cared what the throngs might say
Who passed him unheeding from day to day,
For he only longed with his melodies
The soul of the one beloved to please.

The song of war that he sang is as naught
For the field and its heroes are long forgot,
And the song he sang of fame and power
Was never remembered beyond its hour!
Only to-day his name is known
By the song he sang apart and alone.
And the great world pauses with joy to hear
The notes that were strung for a lover's ear.

(1908)

Not ours to join in the well-fought fray
   Where the stout blows ring and the good shields quiver,
Not ours to grasp on this lavish day
   The victory guerdoned by fame forever!
Nay, it is ours to stand and wait
Till the shadows are long and the eve is late,
In prayerful patience to dwell aside
While others forth to the conflict ride.

We who wait may be sad and stern
   As the lagging years creep whitely o'er us,
Doing our duty with hearts that burn
   For the wide red field and the kindling chorus;
But reward will come, and this may it be –
To grapple yet with the enemy,
And win the boon of the waiting past
In the right to *one* valiant blow at last!

(1914)

Bride of a day, your eye is bright,
   And the flower of your cheek is red.
"He died with a smile on a field of France –
   I smile for his sake," she said.

Mother of one, the babe you bore
   Sleeps in a chilly bed.
"He gave himself with a gallant pride –
   Shall I be less proud?" she said.

Woman, you weep and sit apart,
   Whence is your sorrow fed?
"I have none of love or kin to go –
   I am shamed and sad," she said.

(1918)

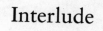

Interlude

We were out on the hills that night
   To watch our sheep;
Drowsily by the fire we lay
    Where the waning flame did flicker and leap,
   And some were weary and half asleep,
And some talked low of their flocks and the fright
   Of a lion that day.

But I had drawn from the others apart;
   I was only a lad,
And the night's great silence so filled my heart
   That I dared not talk and I dared not jest;
The moon had gone down behind the hill,
And even the wind of the desert was still;
As the touch of death the air was cold,
And the world seemed all outworn and old;
   Yet a poignant delight in my soul was guest,
   And I could not be sad.

Still were my thoughts the thoughts of youth
   Under the skies;
I dreamed of the holy and tender truth
   That shone for me in my mother's eyes;
Of my little sister's innocent grace,
And the mirthful lure in the olive face
Of a maid I had seen at the well that day,
Singing low as I passed her way;
And so sweet and wild were the notes of her song
   That I listened long.

Was it the dawn that silvered and broke
   Over the hill?
Each at the other looked in amaze,

And never a breathless word we spoke.
    Fast into rose and daffodil
Deepened that splendor; athwart its blaze
    That pierced like a sword the gulf of night
    We saw a Form that was shaped of the light,
And we veiled our faces in awe and dread
    To hearken the tidings the Bright One told –
O, wonderful were the words he said –
    Of a Child in Bethlehem's manger old.

The stars were drowned in that orient glow;
    The sky was abloom like a meadow in spring;
But each blossom there was a radiant face,
    And each flash of glory a shining wing;
They harped of peace and great good will,
And such was their music that well I know
There can never again in my soul be space
    For a sound of ill.

The light died out as the sunset dies
In the western skies;
Swift went we to the Bethlehem khan.
Many our questions laughed to scorn;
But one, a gray and wrinkled man
    With strange, deep eyes that searched the heart,
Led us down to the Child new-born
    In a dim-lighted cave apart.

There on the straw the mother lay
    Wan and white,
But her look was so holy and rapt and mild
    That it seemed to shed a marvellous light,
Faint as the first rare gleam of day,
    Around the child.

It was as other children are
    Saving for something in the eyes,
    Starlike and clear and strangely wise.
There came a sudden thought to me

Of a lamb I had found on the waste afar,
Lost and sick with hunger and cold;
I had brought it back in my arms to the fold
    For tender ministry.

Dawn had flooded the east as a wave
When we left the cave;
    All the world suddenly seemed to be
Young and pure and joyous again;
The others lingered to talk with the men,
Full of wonder and rapture still;
But I hastened back to the fold on the hill
    To tend the lamb that had need of me.

(1908)

Songs of Land and Sea

WHEN THE FISHING BOATS GO OUT

When the pearly skies of morning flush with dawning rose once
    more,
And waves of golden glory break along the sunrise shore,
And o'er the arch of heaven white wings of vapor float,
There's rapture and there's freedom when the fishing-boats go
    out.

The wind is blowing freshly up from far-off ocean caves,
And sending sparkling kisses o'er the brows of virgin waves,
While routed dawn-mists shiver and fast and far they flee,
Pierced by the shafts of sunrise and the glitter of the sea.

Behind us fair, light-smitten hills in new-born splendor lie,
Before us the wide ocean sweeps to meet the morning sky,
Our hearts are full of seething life and care has fled afar,
As sweeps the white-winged fishing-fleet across the harbor bar.

The sea is calling to us in a joyous voice and free –
There's keenest rapture on its breast, and boundless liberty!
Each man is master of his craft, its gleaming sails outblown,
And far behind him on the shore a home he calls his own.

Salt is the breath of ocean slopes and fresher blows the breeze,
And swifter still each bounding keel cuts thro' the crowding
    seas.
Athwart our masts the shadows of the dipping seagulls float,
And all the water-world's alive when the fishing-boats go out.

(1899)

The sea dusk shrouds in violet gloom the ocean's silver blue,
And purple headlands whence, at dawn, the milk-white sea-
    gulls flew;
The dances of the wild night-winds o'er glimmering sweeps
    begin,
And the sun sinks down on a couch of fire when the fishing
    boats come in.

The glorious arch of sky above is faintly filmed o'er
With silk-white scarfs of vapor, and along the sunset shore
Vast cloud-fleets ride at anchor in seas of gold and rose,
While with a trembling splendor the wide horizon glows.

The murmurous roar of far-off deep blends with the plaintive
    sigh
Of wavelets that upon the sands of gleaming silver die;
The darkling cliffs loom out behind, like giants vast and grim,
Stern guardians of enchanted coasts enwrapped in shadows
    dim.

Like some great jewel burns the sea and on its gleaming breast
The laden, home-bound boats glide o'er each shimmering,
    foam-belled crest.
Glad watchers scan each glowing sail, fond eyes are straining
    still,
And with the stir of fearless life the dusk is all athrill.

A hearty shout goes up to greet the latest furling sail,
The long shore rings with mirth and joy, the ocean glimmers
    pale;
A sea-bird flies athwart the sky and from the fading west
One lingering rose-red ray outflames to crimson wing and
    breast.

The winds are revelling o'er the reefs, the rocky sea-deeps
   moan,
The silken slopes are dim and far, the fishing grounds are lone;
The sparkles of the mirrored stars among the ripples spin,
And the shore is gemmed with a hundred lights when the fish-
   ing boats come in.

(1899)

RAIN IN THE WOODS

I.

Just a hush among the trees –
    Do the woods a-listening stand?
Silent all the melodies,
    Gone the wandering winds that fanned
Beechen crests and piney cones,
    All the sylvan sounds that spanned
Wood and hill with faintest tones.

II.

Then there come the drops of rain,
    Rustling through the leafy screen,
With a tinkling, wild refrain,
    Mossy trunks and boughs between;
Splashing on the shadowed brook,
    Damping grass and mosses green
Growing in each dusky nook.

III.

Moist and odorous grows the air
    With the breath of dripping flowers,
And the pungent fragrance rare
    Ferns distil in summer showers.
Nature has a hundred moods,
    But her rarest are the hours
When the rain falls in the woods.

(1899)

MY PICTURES

My pictures? Why, yes; I will show them with gladness –
   Their number is small, but each one is a gem;
And in shadow or sunshine they charm away sadness,
   The world is forgotten while gazing at them.

They were painted, each one, by the hand of a master
   Whose skill is unquestioned, whose brush is most true,
Whose colors are brighter, whose canvasses vaster
   Than any, my friend, that are cherished by you.

See! There is a valley that's dappled with shadow
   And threaded with sunshine, in bosk and in dell;
Or here, if you like, is a green stretch of meadow
   A-twinkle with daisies where buttercups dwell.

Here's a garden of blossom, an orchard bloom-whitened,
   And others beyond that I need not to name,
All seen at a glance when the summer has brightened
   The scenes that I view from my own window frame.

(1906)

THE WIND IN THE POPLARS

I.

Sad and strange as some weird old rune,
  Hark to the wind in the poplar trees!
Always the same low, haunting croon,
  As if it dreamed of old memories
In the dim gray twilight, when, soft and deep,
  The sunset fades in the distant west –
For the wind in the poplars can never sleep,
  Its sorrowful threnody knows no rest.

II.

Tall and sombre the poplars stand,
  Like the priestly forms of a mystic band;
Ever their silent watch they keep
  Around the old house in the hours of sleep.
And ever the wind in the still night-time
Rings through their branches its quaint old chime,
And sobs and moans through the quivering leaves
Like some wandering spirit that ceaseless grieves.

III.

Listen! I hear it – faint and low,
  As if it were lulled to a broken rest;
Only a murmur to and fro
  Lightly stirs in each airy crest.
Surely the wind has gone to sleep
And no longer its mournful tryst will keep.
Nay, it comes with a sudden rush –
  Tossing the branches athwart the sky,
Breaking the spell of the evening hush
  And the solemn stars with its phantom cry.
Still, through it all rings a wild refrain;
Rapt exultation is blent with pain,

As its fingers waken mad melodies –
O! how the wind loves the poplar trees!

IV.

It whispers to them in its airy speech
   Of mystic lore and forgotten things,
The sibylline truths that the midnights teach,
   And weird and lonely imaginings.
Hark again to its dreamy croon,
   Dying away into silence brief,
And anon it murmurs a gentler tone,
   Half of rapture and half of grief.
Restless wind in the poplars' crest,
How your threnodies lull my rest!
How I should miss in the solemn night
Your voice like the voice of a lost delight!

V.

Still it chants in the twilight gray,
   Among the shadows that flit and creep,
When the rose-light has died from the sky away
   And their tireless vigil the poplars keep.
Wild is the music – strange and wild –
   Elfin laughter and fitful moan,
Sorrowful cadence and murmur mild,
   Are blent together in every tone.
Yet there's ever a charm in the broken strain,
And a spirit voice in the old refrain,
And never were sweeter fugues than these
The night wind plays in the poplar trees.

(1906)

THE SEA-SHELL

Where the old shores were purple a glossy sea-shell lying
    Upon the pale sands listened to the rune of long gray seas,
And far from its birth-billows now forevermore 'tis sighing
    And dreamlike crooning to itself those vagrant melodies.

List here – the harp-notes of the wind in morning skies of
      amber,
    And now the boom of breakers on some sweep of sundown
      lea,
And now the song the ripples sang in every iris chamber,
    A merry lilt o' moonlight for mermaiden revelry!

Oh, faithful is the heart of it to all dear haunts of ocean,
    And evermore we hear in it the magic of their spell,
Nor time nor inland exile can mar its fond devotion,
    Forever sung unwearied in the singing of the shell!

(1909)

BEFORE STORM

There's a grayness over the harbour like fear on the face of a
   woman,
   The sob of the waves has a sound akin to a woman's cry,
And the deeps beyond the bar are moaning with evil presage
   Of a storm that will leap from its lair in that dour northeast-
   ern sky.

Slowly the pale mists rise, like ghosts of the sea, in the offing,
   Creeping all wan and chilly by headland and sunken reef,
And a wind is wailing and keening like a lost thing 'mid the
   islands,
   Boding of wreck and tempest, plaining of dolour and grief.

Swiftly the boats come homeward, over the grim bar crowding,
   Like birds that flee to their shelter in a hurry and affright,
Only the wild gray gulls that love the cloud and the clamour
   Will dare to tempt the ways of the ravening sea to-night.

But the ship that sailed at the dawning, manned by the lads that
   love us,
   God help and pity her when the storm is looséd on her track!
Oh, women, we pray to-night and keep a vigil of sorrow
   For those we sped at the dawning and may never welcome
   back!

(1909)

A SHORE PICTURE

A windy, hollow sky of crystal clear,
   Scarfed with a fringe of sunset in the west,
A dim sail gliding by the headland near,
   And, hung above the purpling fir-wood's crest,
A great gold star, like some calm acolyte
That watches steadfast by the gulf of night.

An argosy of crimson cloud at sea
   Pennoned with primrose, and, beyond the dune,
Pallid as any fast-worn devotee,
   The wan face of a lately risen moon
Above a landward valley whose deep cup
With dewy, placid twilight is brimmed up.

Far out, foam wreaths as wavering and as white
   As some cold sea-maid's gleaming arms uptossed
Athwart the splendours of the afterlight –
   Seen for a moment, then forever lost –
And at our feet long waves that evermore
Lap silver-tongued upon the burnished shore.

(1910)

Lo, I have loved thee long, long have I yearned and entreated!
   Tell me how I may win thee, tell me how I must woo.
Shall I creep to thy white feet, in guise of a humble lover?
   Shall I croon in mild petition, murmuring vows anew?

Shall I stretch my arms unto thee, biding thy maiden coyness,
   Under the silver of morning, under the purple of night?
Taming my ancient rudeness, checking my heady clamor –
   Thus, is it thus I must woo thee, oh, my delight?

Nay, 'tis no way of the sea thus to be meekly suitor –
   I shall storm thee away with laughter wrapped in my beard
      of snow,
With the wildest of billows for chords I shall harp thee a song
      for thy bridal,
   A mighty lyric of love that feared not nor would forego!

With a red-gold wedding ring, mined from the caves of sunset,
   Fast shall I bind thy faith to my faith evermore,
And the stars will wait on our pleasure, the great north wind
      will trumpet
   A thunderous marriage march for the nuptials of sea and
      shore.

(1916)

Songs of Death

When she was dead
They came and brought the roses pale and fair
To twine within her thin and silver hair;
They softly laid white lilies on her breast
Where her poor weary hands were crossed in rest.
Though while she lived they never sent a flower
To whisper comfort in a darksome hour,
They decked with blossoms beautiful her bed
When she was dead.

When she was dead
They said her life had been so true and grand;
They told how many times her helping hand
Had aided them in trouble – how she brought
Sunshine and cheer to many a gloomy lot,
And how her fingers always seemed to be
Toiling for others uncomplainingly.
They said her days in kindness had been sped
When she was dead.

When she was dead
They spoke not of her faults. They murmured low
Of all sweet virtues she was wont to show.
They said that love and pity were her creed
And blessed her for each kindly word and deed.
They wondered as they kissed her through their tears
How they could live without her through the years.
Oh, many kind and tender things they said
When she was dead.

And she was dead!
The heart their loving speech would once have thrilled
With thankful gladness was forever stilled.

In life she sought their love and seldom heard
In all her busy days one grateful word,
And now it was too late they came and knelt
Beside her, telling all they thought and felt.
She could not hear the longed-for words they said
For she was dead.

(1901)

I have buried my dead –
    And so I come to you!
Will you be comforted
    By one who has suffered, too?
I know what it is –
    The longing and the pain –
Well have I learned to miss
    One who comes not again.
I can feel with you:
    I have buried my dead!

They may pity you
    Who have not felt the sting,
But sympathy deep and true
    Comes but on suffering's wing.
How can they know who ne'er
    Have watched the failing breath,
Or knelt with anguished prayer
    At the very gates of death?
But I – I know –
    I have buried my dead!

I know how you miss
    The footfall on the floor,
How you yearn for the kiss
    And the hand you clasp no more;
How the long night through
    The bitterness is so deep
That its sorrow follows you
    Even in troubled sleep.
Yes, I know –
    I have buried my dead!

Here with you will I stay
   And I will hold your hand;
Not a word will I say
   But you will understand.
Heart that speaks to heart
   Needeth not human speech
Sympathy to impart;
   Grief will a language teach.
I have learned it well –
   I have buried my dead!

(1901)

OMEGA

I am to die to-night! A solemn calm
Falls on my spirit like a tranquil balm.
Long ere the dawn my soul will take its flight
Beyond the purple battlements of night,
Beyond the fading sunset's golden bar,
Beyond the gateway of the evening star,
      For I go out to-night.

Once I have dreamed when this dark hour drew near
That I would shudder with unlanguaged fear.
I thought my soul would shrink the vast Unknown
O'er whose dim boundaries it must speed alone.
But now – I cannot tell – I know not why –
It does not seem a fearsome thing to die,
      And that to-night.

The dim past fades like some receding dream;
Success – ambition – now how frail they seem!
Elusive phantoms of a world gone by
That have no power to hold my fading eye.
Love, hatred, hope and fear – all, all are o'er,
Passion has power to wring my heart no more –
      I am to die to-night.

To-night, this very night, I shall know more
Than all the ages boast of gone before!
I shall be wiser than all living men;
No mystery will be beyond my ken,
And my freed soul with undimmed eyes shall see
The awful secrets of eternity,
      To-night – to-night!

To-night – strange thought! – I shall behold once more,
Changed or unchanged, the friends I lost of yore.
Haply they may not know me, or have passed
Into some higher radiance, great and vast,
Where I, as yet earth-blinded, may not go,
Or they may still be mine – but I shall know
        After to-night.

Truth shall be mine at last – the truth I sought
In creeds and systems now remembered not,
Or dimly. Prove the knowledge what it may,
Death were for such a boon small price to pay!
Strange awe is mine, but fear and grief are past,
For I have reached the bourne of time at last,
        And I go out to-night!

(1903)

Make it where the winds may sweep
Through the pine boughs soft and deep,
And the murmur of the sea
Come across the Orient lea,
And the falling rain-drops sing
Gently to his slumbering.

Make it where the meadows wide
Greenly lie on every side,
Harvest fields he reaped and trod,
Westering slopes of clover sod,
Orchard lands where bloom and blow
Trees he planted long ago.

Make it where the starshine dim
May be always close to him,
And the sunrise glory spread
Lavishly around his bed,
And the dewy grasses creep
Tenderly above his sleep.

Since these things to him were dear
Through full many a well-spent year,
It is surely meet their grace
Should be on his resting-place,
And the murmur of the sea
Be his dirge eternally.

(1906)

These I may not take with me:
Gems that sparkle lustrously,
Gold hard won with toil and tears
Through my many busy years,
Fertile meadows stretching wide,
Mansions decked with splendid pride;
Mine they are, but well I know
I must leave them when I go.

These things I may take with me
Into immortality:
The affection undefiled
Of a little pure-eyed child,
Blessing that a beggar spoke
When my crust of bread he broke,
Prayer a friend made fervently;
These things I may take with me.

(1907)

Songs of Love

If love should come,
  I wonder if my restless, troubled heart,
  Unkind, would bid its visitor depart,
    With chill, averted look and pulse enthralled,
    Because its sanctum was already filled
By cold ambition – would it still be dumb
      If love should come?

If love should come,
  Would all his pleading fall upon my ear
  Unrecked of, as by one who will not hear?
    Would my lips say, "I do not know thy name;
    I seek the far, cold heights where dwelleth fame.
In all my life for thee there is no room,"
      If love should come?

If love should come,
  Against him would I dare to bar the door,
  And, unregretful, bid him come no more?
    Would stern ambition whisper to my heart,
    "Love is a weakness – bid him hence depart,
For he and I can have no common home,"
      If love should come?

If love should come,
  And I should shut him out and turn away,
  Would what contents me now content me aye?
    Would all success the lonely years might bring
    Suffice to recompense for that one thing?
Ah, *could* my heart be silent, my lips dumb,
      If love should come?

(1897)

ASSURANCE

Well, we have parted, you and I – and you
　　Think that our dream of love is past forever,
Nor know, as I do, that the spell I threw
　　Across your life no power can wholly sever,
And through all time, altho' to-day we part,
Something of me will linger in your heart.

The songs I sang you when our love was new,
　　The words I murmured when your arms caressed me,
My eyes aglow with tenderness for you,
　　My happy sigh as to your heart you pressed me,
Will all come back, wherever you may be,
At fitful hours and you will think of me.

The tender kisses from my red lips won
　　Will sweeter seem than all that others give you,
And though you deem our time of loving done,
　　The memory of its bliss will never leave you.
I know – and in the knowledge drown my pain –
You'll never love, as you loved me, again.

And so – good-by! I would not have you stay
　　If you would go, new raptures to discover –
Yet be assured that – find what you may –
　　You will not find so fond and true a lover
As I have been – and always you will know
Deep in your heart of hearts that this is so.

(1900)

Folded away in the cedar chest,
  Carefully hid from the garish day,
In an inviolate, perfumed rest
  Lies that dainty gown of glistening gray –
Never again to be worn by her
In its silvery splendor, its silken stir,
  A garment meet for loveliness,
For her face was fair as the buds of spring,
And her girlish voice had a blithesome ring,
  That half was laughter and half caress.

As I saw her then I can see her now
  When last she wore it – the soft, brown hair
Curling and creeping around a brow
  Pure as a lily and thrice as fair;
And the long-lashed eyes of that flawless blue
Of the sky at eve, when the stars shine through,
  And the face like a sweet, flushed rose abloom;
The red-ripe lips and the dimpled hands –
I am not sure but again she stands
  Here as of old in this dim-lit room.

How she nestled against my heart that day,
  My heart that throbbed with unlanguaged bliss!
I held her close in her silken gray,
  My lips still burn with her clinging kiss
As to her rose-mouth my own was pressed;
The little brown head lay on my breast,
  The little soft arms were about me thrown –
Ah, it was all in the far, sweet past,
Such measureless happiness could not last,
  My heart is empty, my life is lone.

Fold it with reverent touch away,
    Gently fasten the cedarn lid;
In the lustrous, faint-scented folds of gray
    Let the sweet dead dream of my life lie hid!
Leave it here in this quaint old room,
Wrapped in the shroud of its dusky gloom,
    This gown that she wore so long ago.
Who will believe that to-day she came
Back from the past to me, just the same?
    The world would laugh lightly, but I – I know!

(1903)

She's standing on the bridge above me looking down
    Lovelier than e'er I thought her!
Now a smile comes o'er her face and now a frown
    Like the lights and shadows on the water.
        While I at leisure float
        Below her in my boat
Wondering what motive here has brought her.

Has she come here by design, or just by chance,
    Or to watch the waters shiver
Round the reeds that bend, or wave-caught sunbeams dance
    At the bend there in the river?
        Or do those willful eyes
        Watch the foam-bubbles rise
Where the breezes fret the wavelets till they quiver?

Does she guess the charming picture she makes there
    Bending just a little over?
One white hand to hold her hat upon her hair,
    While a saucy ringlet plays the rover
        Across her dimpled cheek!
        What if I dared to speak
Ere she goes and tell her how I love her?

Still she's standing on the bridge and looking down
    With her face turned o'er her shoulder.
I wonder if 'twould be a smile or frown
    That would greet me if I told her.
        I think I'll moor the boat
        Where the long grasses float
And go up on the bridge for I've grown bolder!

(1904)

GRATITUDE

I thank thee, friend, for the beautiful thought
    That in words well-chosen thou gavest to me.
Deep in the life of my soul it has wrought
    With its own rare essence to ever imbue me –
To gleam like a star over devious ways,
To bloom like a flower on the dreariest days.
Better such gift from thee to me
Than gold of the hills or pearls of the sea.

For the luster of jewels and gold may depart
    And they have in them no life of the giver,
But this gracious gift from thy heart to my heart
    Shall witness to me of thy love forever!
Yea, it shall always abide with me
As a part of my immortality,
For a beautiful thought is a thing divine,
So I thank thee, O friend, for this gift of thine!

(1907)

With tears they buried you to-day,
  But well I knew no turf could hold
  Your gladness long beneath the mould,
Or cramp your laughter in the clay;
I smiled while others wept for you,
Because I knew.

And now you sit with me to-night,
  Here in our old, accustomed place;
  Tender and mirthful is your face;
Your eyes with starry joy are bright.
Oh, you are merry as a song,
For love is strong!

They think of you as lying there,
  Down in the churchyard grim and old;
  They think of you as mute and cold,
A wan, white thing that once was fair,
With dim, sealed eyes that never may
Look on the day.

But love cannot be coffined so
  In clod and darkness; it must rise
  And seek its own in radiant guise,
With immortality aglow,
Making of death's triumphant sting
A little thing.

Ay, we shall laugh at those who deem
  Our hearts are sundered! Listen, sweet:
  The tripping of the wind's swift feet,
Along the byways of our dream,

And hark the whisper of the rose
Wilding that blows.

Oh, still you love those simple things,
  And still you love them more with me;
  The grave has won no victory;
It could not clasp your shining wings;
It could not keep you from my side,
Dear and my bride!

(1914)

FOREVER

I.

With you I shall ever be;
Over land and sea
My thoughts will companion you;
With yours shall my laughter chime,
And my step keep time
In the dusk and dew
With yours in blithesome rhyme;
In all of your joy shall I rejoice,
On my lips your sorrow shall find a voice,
And when your tears in bitterness fall
Mine shall mingle with them all;
With you in waking and dream I shall be,
In the place of shadow and memory,
Under young springtime moons,
And on harvest noons,
And when the stars are withdrawn
From the white pathway of the dawn.

II.

O, my friend, nothing shall ever part
My soul from yours, yours from my heart!
I am yours and you mine, in silence and in speech,
Death will only seal us each to each.
Through the darkness we shall fare with fearless jest,
Starward we shall go on a joyous new quest;
There be many worlds, as we shall prove,
Many suns and systems, but only one love!

(1916)

TO ONE HATED

"Hate is only Love that has missed its way."

Had it been when I came to the valley where the paths parted
    asunder,
    Chance had let my feet to the way of love, not hate,
I might have cherished you well, have been to you fond and
    faithful,
    Great as my hatred is, so might my love have been great.

Each cold word of mine might have been a kiss impassioned,
    Warm with the throb of my heart, thrilled with my pulse's
    leap,
And every glance of scorn, lashing, pursuing, and stinging,
    As a look of tenderness would have been wondrous and
    deep.

Bitter our hatred is, old and strong and unchanging,
    Twined with the fibres of life, blent with body and soul,
But as its bitterness, so might have been our love's sweetness
    Had it not missed the way – strange missing and sad! – to its
    goal.

(1916)

You ask me when I loved you first?
   For years, sweetheart, before you came
Your ideal in my heart was nursed
   And worshiped with a holy flame;
Dear, when you took your waiting throne
You simply came into your own.

Why do I love you? For the sweet,
   Shy glances of down-drooping eyes,
For smiles and laughter fairy-fleet,
   For words and whispers fondly wise;
And, truer than all reasons true,
Because, my lady, you are *you*.

And will I always love you so?
   But yea, my winsome catechist,
As long as Aprils come and go,
   And springtime violets keep their tryst;
Yet, ask it often as you will
Because I joy to answer still.

(1921)

Postlude

THE POET

There was strength in him and the weak won freely from it,
  There was an infinite pity, and hard hearts grew soft thereby,
There was truth so unshrinking and starry-shining,
  Men read clear by its light and learned to scorn a lie.

His were songs so full of a wholesome laughter
  Those whose courage was ashen found it once more aflame,
His was a child-like faith and wandering feet were guided,
  His was a hope so joyous despair was put to shame.

His was the delicate insight and his the poignant vision
  Whereby the world might learn what wine-lipped roses
    know,
What a drift of rain might lisp on a gray sea-dawning,
  Or a pale spring of the woodland babble low.

He builded a castle of dream and a palace of rainbow fancy,
  And the starved souls of his fellows lived in them and grew
    glad; –
And yet – there were those who mocked the gifts of his gener-
  ous giving,
  And some – but he smiled and forgave them – who deemed
    him wholly mad!

(1916)

Coda

Life, as thy gift I ask no rainbow joy
Through all my years, lest I grow hard and cold,
Empty of tenderness. Nay, rather, Life,
Give me to know of sorrow; let me win
From sacred pain a loftier heritage
Than any heired by gladness; let me hold
Remembrance of thy suffering, knowing well
The root is bitter but the blossom sweet;
Life, thy great lessons must be hardly learned;
I pray thee, spare me not a single line
Or a strait problem for my weariness;
Teach me, if need be, by the dint of scourge,
That at the last I may have learned them all,
Nor lost some precious portion of thy lore
Through a weak wish for present joy and ease.

(1912)

Afterword

With one side of her nature she liked writing prose best –
with the other she liked writing poetry.

– *EMILY CLIMBS*[1]

"POETRY WAS MY FIRST LOVE AND I HAVE ALWAYS RE-
gretted being false to it. But one must live." With this
statement – one that evokes youthful passion, lament, betrayal,
financial crisis, and survival – L.M. Montgomery concluded a
piece entitled "An Autobiographical Sketch."[2] By the time she
published this essay in 1929, she had been a bestselling novelist
for over two decades, ever since the publication of her first book,
Anne of Green Gables (1908), which had established both her
popularity and her critical reputation. Her astonishing success as
a novelist, compounded with marriage to a minister and a move
from her native Prince Edward Island to rural Ontario in 1911
as well as motherhood starting in 1912, led to a set of social and
personal expectations that would constrain her creative freedom
for the rest of her life. As she explained in a 1926 letter to her
correspondent Ephraim Weber, using language that anticipated
the published essay of three years later, "Writing verse was my
first love and I always hanker after it but I never can get time
for it."[3]

Still, Montgomery's sense of herself as having been "false" to
this first literary love is complicated by the fact that she had
published more than 450 poems by the late 1920s, with another
two dozen to follow by the time of her death in 1942, in addition
to an even higher number of short stories. If anything, it was the

magazine market that had driven Montgomery to be false to poetry, at least as far as her ability to earn a living was concerned. In a 1903 letter to her correspondent G.B. MacMillan, she understated her literary ambitions by recasting them in terms of dollars and cents. Stating that "I am frankly in literature to make my living out of it" – a declaration that clashes with expressions of ambition that she had framed in her journal and later in a celebrity memoir using the metaphor of "the Alpine Path"[4] – she articulated the difficulty she had of finding a balance between literary integrity and the reality of earning a living with her pen: "I know that I touch a far higher note in my verse than in prose. But I write much more prose than verse because there is a wider market for it." She added that in the preceding year she had "made $500 by writing of which less than $100 came from verse."[5] This discrepancy in terms of earnings and modes of writing – which should not be surprising given that many periodicals paid authors a flat fee per word – was largely unchanged when, in a ledger now housed at the University of Guelph archives, she did an accounting, dated 7 February 1921, of her lifetime earnings as a writer and determined that she had earned an average of $3.45 per poem, compared to an average of $13.14 per short story. In the last of several updates in this ledger, dated 13 February 1939, her average rate had roughly doubled to $28.55 per short story but had stayed largely the same at $3.80 per poem.[6] Far from being "false" to poetry, she continued to write it because doing so satisfied her creatively, if not financially.

But it is important to acknowledge that, while the creative benefit was considerable, Montgomery's large output of poems was published in and, to a point, written for a wide range of mainstream North American periodicals – faith-based or secular, urban or rural, targeting general or specific readerships – that were run by editors looking for material that would appeal to large numbers of readers.[7] And as the ongoing digitization of historical print materials is making increasingly apparent, a significant proportion of her periodical work recirculated in innumerable newspapers across the continent, often possibly without her knowledge, let alone her consent. What this means is that she had to find the balance between creative satisfaction and the demands of the mass market as they evolved over a fifty-year period. As she stated in a 1902 journal entry quoted in "The Alpine

Path" concerning a week in the life of a professional writer, "I
have ground out several blameless rhymes for a consideration of
filthy lucre and I have written one *real* poem out of my heart"
– without identifying which were which.[8] In this sense, she differs
from the Confederation Poets – Charles G.D. Roberts (1860–
1943), Bliss Carman (1861–1929), Archibald Lampman (1861–
1899), and Duncan Campbell Scott (1862–1947) – and their
contemporaries Ethelwyn Wetherald (1857–1940), S. Frances
Harrison (1859–1935), and E. Pauline Johnson/Tekahionwake
(Mohawk) (1861–1913), all of whom published multiple volumes of verse and whose poems have recirculated far more
widely than Montgomery's, both within their lifetimes and in
the years since their deaths.[9] As Carole Gerson notes in a chapter on the business practices of early women writers in Canada,
"While money was often to be made from periodicals, prestige
and canonicity have been conferred by books," given that, "as
the vehicle of cultural preservation, the book confers a sense of
permanence upon an author or her work."[10] Partly because most
of Montgomery's poems have been lost in the pages of old periodicals, they remain among her least-known contributions to
literature.

Moreover, Montgomery's few attempts to circulate her poems
beyond the fleeting magazine market were fraught with com-
plications, one of which was that she rarely mentioned these
attempts in her surviving life writing. Sometime around 1903,
in the early years of her freelance career, she self-published a
chapbook of thirty-two poems that was apparently intended for
distribution among friends and family members, but she left no
record of it in her journals, let alone any indication of how many
copies she had printed or what her expectations were concerning
its circulation. She likewise did not make any explicit mention of
the project to either MacMillan or Weber, even though she was
usually forthright about acceptances of her work in periodicals
and both men had been eager to correspond with her because
they had admired her poetry.[11] In fact, if it was not for the
three surviving copies of this untitled and undated poetry chapbook – now housed at Library and Archives Canada, the L.M.
Montgomery Collection at the University of Guelph archives,
and the Thomas Fisher Rare Book Library at the University of
Toronto – I am not certain we would know of its existence.

In 1916, after publishing seven books of fiction with
L.C. Page and Company of Boston, four of which featured Anne,
Montgomery left that firm due to a number of grievances, among
them Page's unwillingness to publish a volume of her poems on
the grounds that it would not be financially profitable. This
refusal would have stung, not only because Montgomery had
been enthusiastic about publishing her first novel with Page on
the grounds that he had "published several successful books by
well-known authors, including Charles G.D. Roberts and Bliss
Carman,"[12] but also because he had already made a fortune on
the sales of her six novels and one collection of linked short stories. She switched that year to joint publication by McClelland,
Goodchild, and Stewart (later McClelland and Stewart) in
Toronto and the Frederick A. Stokes Company in New York,
in part because of the willingness of both firms to publish a book
of her poems in order to obtain the rights to her next novel,
Anne's House of Dreams, which would appear in August 1917;
that arrangement with these two publishers would continue for
the remainder of her career. Published in November 1916, *The
Watchman and Other Poems* contains ninety-four poems (most
of them first published in periodicals between 1899 and 1916),
and while it received largely favourable reviews,[13] it did not reach
nearly as wide an audience as her book-length fiction did; in fact,
in her February 1921 tally of lifetime earnings as an author, she
noted that *Watchman* had earned her $139.12, whereas *Anne's
House of Dreams* had earned her $16,456.26 by that point.[14]
Although Montgomery recorded in her journal upon receipt of
her author's copies of her poetry collection that she "expect[ed]
no great things of it," leading Susan Fisher to suggest that this
"apparent indifference to the fate of *The Watchman* may reflect
her assessment of her own talent," Mary Henley Rubio argues
that Montgomery had been "deeply involved with this book on
an emotional level." Rubio also suggests that the book's title alludes to "the highest sand dune on the Cavendish shore," which
would link the title of this book to those of Montgomery's novels
in terms of their evocation of place.[15]

As further evidence of Montgomery's attachment to her poetry, near the end of her life she attempted to marry her poems to
her always profitable Anne characters by creating a final sequel
to *Anne of Green Gables* that blended short fiction, poetry, and

dialogue. Of particular interest are vignettes in which Anne and members of her family discuss forty-one of Montgomery's poems, which in this sequel are attributed to Anne and to her second son, Walter.[16] Entitled *The Blythes Are Quoted* and apparently submitted to her publishers the day of her death in April 1942, it was not published in its entirety until 2009, more than three and a half decades after the publication of a truncated version of the book – one that cut all of the vignettes and all but one of the poems and that abridged an earlier typescript version – as *The Road to Yesterday* in 1974. Much like with her undated poetry chapbook, no record survives of when she worked on the project or what thinking shaped the final version of the book; likewise, there is no known surviving record that indicates the reasoning of Montgomery's publishers in declining to publish the book at the time of her death.

Given this complex interplay between periodical publication and book publication, the publishing history of Montgomery's poems is worth considering in terms of the competing forces of literary reputation, reader recognition, financial profit, and enduring literary quality, especially when placing her career alongside those of her contemporaries. Gerson reveals that "most volumes and booklets of poetry issued in Canada before 1940 were financed by the author, male or female," whether or not a publisher's imprint appeared on the title page – even the books of poems by Duncan Campbell Scott.[17] The willingness of McClelland, Goodchild, and Stewart to publish Montgomery's poetry in order to obtain the rights to her next Anne novel likely made her the exception to this convention, however. Supposing that she received a standard 10 percent royalty on *Watchman*'s list price of $1.25, her receipt of $139.12 would suggest that she had sold 1,159 copies of the book by 1921.[18] If, by her account, she had received an average of $3.45 per poem within the magazine market by that date, she could have earned an estimated total of $324.30 for the book's ninety-four poems had she published or republished them individually in periodicals. Compare to this Isabella Valancy Crawford (1846–1887), who, according to Catherine Ross, had printed at her own expense one thousand copies of *Old Spookses' Pass, Malcolm's Katie, and Other Poems* (1884), the only book she published within her lifetime. "Only fifty copies were sold," Ross notes, "despite generally favourable reviews." Moreover, although Crawford's "literary reputation is based on her poems, particularly her narrative poems," it was her prose in periodicals that became "the bread-and-butter writing by which she earned her precarious living."[19] As for Bliss Carman, who called the title character of *Anne of Green Gables* "such a delightful little person" shortly after the book's release in 1908, Laurel Boone notes that "while his books of poetry improved his reputation, they did nothing for his bank balance." And while Carman's lifetime output included "over fifty volumes of poetry," George L. Parker suggests that Carman's "poems of lasting merit are limited to a handful of regional verses dealing with the Maritimes and New England."[20] In addition, critics note that the most enduring poems by Roberts, Lampman, and Scott are only a small fraction of those they published in their lifetimes (some of their earliest works in the case of Roberts and Lampman) and that all three men supported the writing of poetry with lucrative day jobs, so financial solvency need not have driven their writing priorities, as they did Montgomery's.[21] Meanwhile, of the four contemporaries of Montgomery who were also bestselling novelists in Canada and who join her as the basis of Clarence Karr's study *Authors and Audiences: Popular Canadian Fiction in the Early Twentieth Century* (2000), Charles W. Gordon ("Ralph Connor," 1860–1937) did not publish poetry, whereas Nellie L. McClung (1873–1951), Arthur Stringer (1874–1950), and Robert J.C. Stead (1880–1959) published poems that are now largely unknown or seen as of limited interest.[22]

Montgomery's work is a bit of an anomaly, then, given that her contributions to literature that were most financially successful during her lifetime – her Anne books – are also the ones that have endured with the public for over a century, supported and extended by adaptations for stage and screen, tourist sites, commodities, and supplementary texts. But while *Anne of Green Gables* is by far her best-known text, appearing today in numerous (some might say innumerable) editions across the children's, adult, and scholarly markets, it would be disingenuous to assume that her remaining books have stayed in print only because of the success of the first, rather than on account of their own literary merits. Then again, Montgomery's name recognition as a novelist surely accounted in part for the apparent sale of over eleven hundred copies of *Watchman* compared to the fifty sold copies of Crawford's book of poems, as would the marketing and publicity efforts of Montgomery's publisher. Meanwhile, Crawford's reputation as a poet was helped by the posthumous publication of John W. Garvin's *The Collected Poems of Isabella Valancy Crawford* in 1905 and by Katherine Hale's critical and biographical anthology of Crawford's work in 1923, and while both Garvin and Hale promoted Montgomery's poetry as well,[23] a posthumous volume of Montgomery's collected poems would have been difficult to put together shortly after her death, partly because of the vast range of places in which they had appeared, and partly because such a volume would have been overshadowed by the continued strong sales of her novels.

Moreover, placing Montgomery's poems alongside those of the Confederation Poets and their contemporaries reveals a lot about shared aesthetics. As D.M.R. Bentley suggests in his chapter on post-Confederation poetry in *The Cambridge History of Canadian Literature* (2009), "The poets of the Confederation group regarded time spent in the natural world as an antidote to the psychological and physical wear and tear inflicted by modern urban life"[24] – a statement that could easily be made about Montgomery's poetry as well as her fiction. Indeed, for John Ferns in an article about Montgomery's poetry published in 1986, reading her poems "is like discovering another Confederation poet even though she is of a slightly later generation. She shares Roberts' Wordsworthianism, his philosophical and moral turn of mind and also his love of Eastern Canadian land – and seascapes. She resembles Carman in her metrical lyricism and Lampman in her Keatsian sensuous dwelling upon the luxuriance of nature."[25] These instances of perceived resemblance are complicated, however, by the fact that Montgomery mentions in her life writing and alludes in her fiction to the work of Wordsworth and Keats exponentially more often than she does the work of any of the Confederation Poets.[26] While she read voraciously and widely all her life, the authors that she claimed had had the most influence on her as a writer and had given her the greatest pleasure as a reader were from the United Kingdom and the United States.[27]

As a poet, Montgomery resembles her Confederation compatriots in another respect as well: most of her book-length works of fiction have a seemingly timeless quality that makes them just as readable today as they were a century ago, whereas her poems are more obviously products of their time. Elizabeth Waterston, writing in *L.M. Montgomery and Canadian Culture* (1999), suggests that "[Montgomery's] poetry has fallen into disregard, not necessarily on its own merits, but largely because of a reversal of opinion about poetry itself" – namely, the shift, in the years surrounding the start of the First World War, from "regularity, rhyme, and easily marked rhythms, and from archetypal topics, prettiness, and 'fairy blossoms,'" to poems that are difficult to memorize due to their "tortuously internalized rhymes and complex, metaphorically inverted, undercut meanings" that appeared during the decades that followed.[28] Waterston's point – that it is less Montgomery's poems than the types of poetry she wrote that are now undervalued – echoes the larger evolution of her critical reputation, as a woman author whose texts focused on young people and (apparently) favoured idealism over realism, throughout her career and in the decades since her death.[29] Scholarship over the past several decades has focused on Montgomery's fiction and life writing and on derivatives of that work on stage and screen and in tourism and commodities;[30] that conversation has ignored her poetry almost entirely, even more than thirty years after the publication of John Ferns and Kevin McCabe's selected volume *The Poetry of Lucy Maud Montgomery* (1987).

Indeed, the most detailed analyses of her poetry to date are from Ferns and McCabe themselves, most of them appearing prior to the publication of their volume, in the midst of their collaborative editorial process. Ferns, who places Montgomery's work "largely in the Victorian-Edwardian style," sees influences not only from the Confederation Poets in Canada but also from "such American romantic-transcendentalist poets as Longfellow, Whittier, and Emerson." While he labels her "a minor poet" due to "her adherence to convention" – an adherence that is unsurprising as well as entirely expected given that she published this work primarily in mainstream periodicals – the decision to organize his and McCabe's volume thematically rather than chronologically stemmed from the belief that, throughout what they saw as her most productive years as a poet (1890 to 1915), "her work does not reveal important changes and developments."[31]

McCabe, whose 1985 article in *Canadian Children's Literature / Littérature canadienne pour la jeunesse* would be reworked into the introduction to his and Ferns's collection, also locates the weaknesses in the work in terms of a more general "decline in interest" in "the routine nature of much 'magazine verse'" of the pre–First World War period:

> Poems on certain set topics – the sea, the seasons, boy's life, courage and endeavour, the family circle, etc. – were used as fillers by popular magazines which were bought chiefly by women, children, and casual readers. The long term effect of producing quantities of verse on a limited number of subjects was often a vague and general style which took refuge in "poetical" phrasing and literary platitudes. Poets such as Tennyson and Masefield who attempted to write verses every day showed a progressive decline in poetic verse and expressiveness. L.M. Montgomery is no exception to the rule that the demand for quantity rather than quality eventually showed itself in repetitiveness and undistinguished work.[32]

More recently, Fisher sees these comments as a refusal on McCabe's part to "address[] outright the limitations of Montgomery's poetry," adding that "it is kind of McCabe to suggest that Montgomery was no less a poet than Masefield or Tennyson on a bad day, but Montgomery herself knew better."[33] Still, it is instructive that unlike Ferns, who sees little change in Montgomery's evolution as a poet, McCabe notes that Montgomery's "earlier poetry is somewhat fresher, before it had become more of a product for the market," although he will not go so far as "to divide [her] poetical work into an early and satisfactory period and a later and unsatisfactory period."[34] McCabe returns to this notion in his reassessment of Montgomery's poems in *The Lucy Maud Montgomery Album* (1999), noting that "if [her] poetry had appeared in book form during 1903 or 1904" – around which time Montgomery is believed to have published her chapbook of poems – "her literary career might have taken an entirely different turn."[35]

Given the vast amount of Montgomery's published life writing now available to us, it is easy, perhaps even tempting, to read her poems in biographical terms, guided by the assumption that Montgomery used poetry, like her journals, as an outlet for less manageable emotions – or, as Fisher notes in her recent discussion of Montgomery's war poetry, "an expression of her deepest spiritual impulses."[36] As Montgomery wrote in a journal entry dated 8 April 1898, in which she narrated in retrospect a nightmarish situation of feeling an intense erotic attraction to a man whom she had no intention of marrying while engaged to another man whom she had no intention of marrying, "I have always found that the writing out of a pain makes it at least bearable." Referring to herself in this entry as "the sister and companion of regret and hopeless longing" – language that seems more fitting for a poem than for a journal entry – she claimed that she "did not, with the part of me that *rules*, *want* to marry" the man to whom she felt intense attraction because she perceived him to be socially and intellectually inferior to her; but she later admitted, almost as an aside, that it was her literary ambition that had been the "real barrier between us."[37] Given that this entry is dated less than six months after an entry in which she mentioned "a poem taken by *Munsey*" in a list of recent acceptances[38] (referring to the publication of "If Love Should Come," in December 1897), it would seem reasonable to treat overlaps between journals and periodical work as evidence that many of her poems are autobiographical. Likewise, it might be productive to read her poems "The Exile" and "The Summons," published shortly after her marriage, as expressions of her yearning for Prince Edward Island from her recent home in Ontario.

But there are limits to a biographical reading of these poems, beginning with the fact that Montgomery's poems addressing female objects of desire, which imply male speakers if we see these poems through a heterosexual lens, are among the most complex in this volume. These male speakers add to several male narrators in her short stories, most of which likewise remain uncollected; moreover, taken together, they add substance to Laura Groening's claim about Montgomery's male speakers in her review of Ferns and McCabe's collection: "When Montgomery writes from the perspective of a female, she creates the dainty word pictures that symbolize the suffocating reality of her own life. When she writes from the perspective of a male, she is free to depict a wider-ranging existence, an existence of action and even heroism."[39] And while Montgomery's novels *Kilmeny of the Orchard* (1910), *Anne of the Island* (1915), *Rilla of Ingleside* (1921), *Emily's Quest* (1927), and *Mistress Pat* (1935) all end with a man and a woman declaring their love for each other, with the promise of wedding bells and happily ever after, even the poems appearing in the section "Songs of Love" approach love from a wider range of angles. "Assurance," "The Gray Silk Gown," and "With Tears They Buried You To-day" focus on love lost; "On the Bridge" involves a male speaker trying to rouse his courage to speak to a woman he has loved from afar; "Gratitude" focuses on the durable love of friendship; "To One Hated" speculates about the close proximity between love and hatred. Another complication in a biographical reading of these poems is that only "Forever" and "The Lover's Catechism" in this section express romantic love as something that endures, but the emotions those poems describe are undercut for today's readers with access to Montgomery's journals by the fact that they were published several years after Montgomery, in accepting Ewan Macdonald's marriage proposal in her thirties, had resigned herself to "a workaday, bread-and-butter happiness" that turned out to be disastrous.[40]

Fisher suggests that "it seems reasonable" to conclude that Gilbert Blythe's unspoken assessment of Walter's poems in *The Blythes Are Quoted* – "Commonplace verse ... but the boy had something in him" – mirrors "Montgomery's assessment of her own."[41] I suspect there is more to this textual moment than Fisher's analysis allows, especially given the way it echoes a more central moment in a much earlier novel, *Emily of New Moon* (1923). In the final chapter of that novel, thirteen-year-old Emily Byrd Starr shares some of her poems with her ill-tempered teacher, Mr. Carpenter, who reads extracts aloud and provides almost consistently damning feedback. What has never been noted before in Montgomery scholarship is that all fourteen extracts from Emily's poems that he quotes aloud appear in identical or near identical form in Montgomery's own poems, except with most of the titles changed. After quoting the opening line of Emily's poem "To Life" – which is identical to the first line of Montgomery's "What I Would Ask of Life," which closes this volume – Mr. Carpenter starts to question its author:

" ... Is that sincere? Is it, girl. Stop and think. *Do* you ask 'no rainbow joy' of life?" ...

"No-o," she answered reluctantly. "I *do* want rainbow joy – lots of it."

"Of course you do. We all do. We don't get it – you won't get it – but don't be a hypocrite enough to pretend you don't want it, even in a sonnet ... "[42]

It is tempting to follow Fisher's lead and to read this kind of intertextuality in biographical terms, as evidence of Montgomery reassessing her own work negatively from the perspective of middle age – even though, unlike Emily's "To Life," "What I Would Ask of Life" is most definitely not a sonnet. Although Montgomery told Weber that "people were never right in saying I was 'Anne' but, *in some respects*, they will be right if they write me down as *Emily*,"[43] in this particular instance, such a reading would align her more closely with Mr. Carpenter than with her title character. Instead, I find it more productive to see this moment as Montgomery's attempt to use her older work as authentic detail for constructing a believable writer-in-embryo as protagonist, in spite of the differences in Emily's and Montgomery's ages as authors of this work, especially given that Emily's writing is not yet shaped by market forces or "filthy lucre," to return to Montgomery's terminology. After all, in *Emily's Quest*, when an adult Emily reads through some of the reviews of her first book, *The Moral of the Rose*, many of the extracts she quotes sound remarkably like those from reviews of her books Montgomery had preserved in scrapbooks and written about in her journal.[44] And while Mr. Carpenter ends up finding "ten good lines out of four hundred," calling the rest "balderdash" – a ratio that is probably more generous than the percentage of poems by the Confederation Poets that remains worthwhile today – it is instructive that he sees this percentage not as a defeat but as a clear reason to carry on: "If at thirteen you can write ten good lines, at twenty you'll write ten times ten – if the gods are kind."[45]

In a journal entry dated February 1921, around the time of her first account of her lifetime earnings as a writer and the publication of the last poem in this volume chronologically, Montgomery made a reference to the act of writing poetry that echoes her first letter to MacMillan. "I have been writing a good deal of verse lately – some of it very good – for me. Poetry was my first love in literature ... I touch a higher note in it than in my prose. I finished quite a long poem the other day – 'The Bride Dreams' – and it is, of its kind, the best thing I've done."[46] If we followed Fisher's assessment of Montgomery's comments, we could conclude that the phrases "for me" and "of its kind" signal a tacit acknowledgment on Montgomery's part that her own talents as a poet had limits. Once again, though, I prefer to read this moment differently, given that the poem in question – first published in *The Canadian Bookman*, an official publication of the Canadian Authors Association, the following year – would become one of the strongest and most compelling in *The Blythes Are Quoted*, in which it is attributed to a middle-aged Anne Blythe.[47] To me, Montgomery's late-career decision to attribute so many of her own poems to Anne – and, more crucially, to revise the continuity of the preceding books in order to make that character a poet throughout her life – shows far more convincingly than Gilbert's lukewarm assessment of Walter's poetry the value that Montgomery saw in hers. And, in much the same way that that final book invites readers to experience the contrast between the late poems and the stories and vignettes that surround them, it is my hope that this current volume, in offering a new sampling of poems, will invite today's readers to reconsider Montgomery's endeavours in the literary mode that she found most creatively satisfying.

BENJAMIN LEFEBVRE

NOTES

1 *EC*, 170.
2 Montgomery, "An Autobiographical Sketch," 258.
3 Montgomery to Weber, 18 July 1926, in *AfGG*, 135.
4 Montgomery derived the phrase "the Alpine Path" from a poem that had appeared in a serial published in *Godey's Lady's Book* (Philadelphia) when she was nine years old and that she had clipped and pasted into one of her scrapbooks (see Epperly, *Imagining Anne*, 127). In 1917, she published a 25,000-word celebrity memoir with that title in *Everywoman's World* (Toronto),

a restored and annotated edition of which appears in *A Name for Herself: Selected Writings, 1891–1917.*

5 Montgomery to MacMillan, 29 December 1903, in *MDMM*, 3.

6 Montgomery, "Book Price Record Book," n.p.

7 The reminder that Montgomery wrote periodical pieces with an eye on the market extends to her short stories as well. As Elizabeth Rollins Epperly suggests, Montgomery "shaped her stories to sell to the periodicals she knew or heard about, and she carefully crafted her own pieces to conform to the formula a particular journal favoured" (Epperly, *The Fragrance of Sweet-Grass*, 4).

8 *NH*, 289. This extract appears in slightly different form in Montgomery, 29 March 1902, in *CJLMM*, 2: 50.

9 The term "Confederation Poets" refers usually to Carman, Lampman, Roberts, and Scott, but Isabella Valancy Crawford, William Wilfred Campbell, and George Frederick Cameron are sometimes included in that nomenclature (see Zichy, "Confederation Poets," 140). Poems by Crawford, Campbell, Roberts, Carman, Lampman, Scott, Johnson, and Wetherald appear in both Wilfred Campbell's *The Oxford Book of Canadian Verse* (1913) and Carole Gerson and Gwendolyn Davies's *Canadian Poetry: From the Beginnings through the First World War* (1994), signalling the perceived enduring quality and cultural significance of the work of these poets throughout the twentieth century. By contrast, Montgomery's poems are omitted from both volumes. For more on post-Confederation Canadian poetry, see Roy Daniells's three chapters in *Literary History of Canada*.

10 Gerson, "The Business of a Woman's Life," 80.

11 For more on this chapbook, see Collins, "L.M. Montgomery's 'Little Booklet of Verse.'"

12 Montgomery to Weber, 2 May 1907, in *GGL*, 52.

13 See the chapter devoted to *The Watchman and Other Poems* in Volume 3 of *The L.M. Montgomery Reader*.

14 Montgomery, "Book Price Record Book," n.p.

15 Montgomery, 11 November 1916, in *LMMCJ*, 1: 254; Fisher, "'Watchman, What of the Night?,'" 95; Rubio, *Lucy Maud Montgomery*, 194.

16 Thirty-four of these poems had been published previously: one in 1903, twenty-eight between 1919 and 1940, and five whose published clippings in one of Montgomery's scrapbooks have not yet been identified. An additional poem, "The Piper," was published

in *Saturday Night* magazine two weeks after Montgomery's death (see "[L.M. Montgomery's Last Poem]"; *BQ*, 3).

17 Gerson, "The Business of a Woman's Life," 82.

18 This estimate does not take into account the fact that both the Canadian edition and the American edition (published by Stokes in 1917) sold the book for $1.25 in their respective currencies, nor can it factor what percentage of these sales came from the UK edition of the book, published by Constable in 1920.

19 Ross, "Crawford, Isabella Valancy," 146.

20 "[Such a Delightful Little Person]," 32; Boone, "Bliss Carman's Pageants," 171; Parker, "Carman, Bliss," 103. Boone notes that Carman's books of poetry, like Montgomery's first seven books of prose, were published by "the rapacious L.C. Page" (Boone, "Bliss Carman's Pageants," 171), meaning that, when Page apparently refused to consider publishing a book of Montgomery's poems because "poetry would not pay" (Montgomery, 21 March 1916, in *LMMCJ*, 1: 220), he would have had a clear precedent in Carman to back up his position.

21 Parker, "Roberts, Sir Charles G.D.," 708; Pollock, "Lampman, Archibald," 423; Wicken, "Scott, Duncan Campbell," 740.

22 Dick Harrison notes that Stringer's creative output included "15 volumes of undistinguished verse and non-fiction prose," whereas Stead's "five volumes of slight, patriotic verse ... are of interest mainly as evidence of Stead's devotion to the imperial vision of the Prairies" (Harrison, "Stringer, Arthur," 775; Harrison, "Stead, Robert J.C.," 771).

23 A total of nine of Montgomery's poems appear in Garvin's anthologies *Canadian Poets* (1916, 1926), *Canadian Poems of the Great War* (1918), and *Canadian Verse for Boys and Girls* (1931); Hale concluded a 1927 profile of Montgomery with two stanzas from her poem "When the Dark Comes Down" (see Hale, "About Canadian Writers").

24 Bentley, "Post-Confederation Poetry," 135.

25 Ferns, "'Rainbow Dreams,'" 30.

26 For instance, Rea Wilmshurst's lists of literary allusions in Montgomery's novels total twenty-nine to the work of Wordsworth, twenty-one to the work of Keats, eleven to the work of Carman, one to the work of Roberts, and none to the work of Scott or Lampman (Wilmshurst, "L.M. Montgomery's Use," 40–43; Wilmshurst, "Quotations and Allusions," 74, 76, 78, 80).

27 See Epperly, *The Fragrance of Sweet-Grass*, 4.

28 Waterston, "Reflection Piece," 77, 81, 82.

29 For an overview of shifts in Montgomery's critical reputation since the publication of *Anne of Green Gables*, see my introductions to all three volumes of *The L.M. Montgomery Reader*.

30 Consider, as just a few examples, the work appearing in the most recent collections of essays: Rita Bode and Lesley D. Clement's *L.M. Montgomery's Rainbow Valleys: The Ontario Years, 1911–1942* (2015), Andrea McKenzie and Jane Ledwell's *L.M. Montgomery and War* (2017), and Rita Bode and Jean Mitchell's *L.M. Montgomery and the Matter of Nature(s)* (2018). For exhaustive bibliographies of Montgomery scholarship, visit L.M. Montgomery Online at https://lmmonline.org.

31 Ferns, "'Rainbow Dreams,'" 29, 34, 30. For the response to Ferns and McCabe's volume, see Lefebvre, "Epilogue," 375–76.

32 McCabe, "Lucy Maud Montgomery," 69.

33 Fisher, "'Watchman, What of the Night?,'" 96.

34 McCabe, "Lucy Maud Montgomery," 76, 74.

35 McCabe, "Budding Poetess," 151.

36 Fisher, "'Watchman, What of the Night?,'" 98.

37 Montgomery, 8 April 1898, in *CJLMM*, 1: 389, 393, 410.

38 Montgomery, 7 October 1897, in *CJLMM*, 1: 382.

39 Groening, "The Poetry of Lucy Maud Montgomery," 7.

40 Montgomery, 12 October 1906, in *CJLMM*, 2: 157. An unsigned response to Montgomery's "If Love Should Come" in the *Arizona Republican* assumes a male speaker in spite of the fact that male pronouns are used in reference to the poem's hypothetical lover: "The poet considers the probability of the admission of love against ambition and the result, when ambition should no longer stir the blood. He sang of an earthly love" (*Arizona Republican* [Phoenix], "Two Songs of Love," 5).

41 Fisher, "'Watchman, What of the Night?,'" 97; *BQ*, 370; ellipsis in original.

42 *ENM*, 343–44.

43 Montgomery to Weber, 19 October 1921, in *AfGG*, 88.

44 *EQ*, 243–47; Montgomery, 1 March 1930, in *SJLMM*, 4: 36–43.

45 *ENM*, 347, 348.

46 Montgomery, 2 February 1921, in *LMMCJ*, 2: 304.

47 *BQ*, 399–402.

Notes

The purpose of the following notes is to identify sources for these poems: publications in North American periodicals, clippings of those publications in her scrapbooks, as well as inclusion in Montgomery's self-published chapbook around 1903 and in her full-length collection, *The Watchman and Other Poems* (1916). Her scrapbooks of clippings of her own work, photocopies of which are numbered 1 to 12 and available at the University of Prince Edward Island and University of Guelph library archives (the originals are housed at the Confederation Centre Art Gallery in Charlottetown), consist of Montgomery's official record of her periodical career, although it is not entirely complete. Also, because she made word choices that were archaic even within her lifetime, here I provide definitions of such terms.

OVERTURE

"The Gable Window" appeared in the Toronto magazine *The Ladies' Journal*; a clipping is in Scrapbook 7, alongside which Montgomery indicates that it was published in April 1897, but a copy of that issue has not yet been located. "Vagrance" is an archaic word referring to the act of wandering idly, sometimes without a home base or a means of support, as in the case of a vagrant. In "The Alpine Path: The Story of My Career," Montgomery referred to her novel *The Story Girl* as "the last book I wrote in my old home by the gable window where I had spent so many happy hours of creation" (*NH*, 297). In July 2017, "The Gable Window" was selected by Project Bookmark Canada, an organization that celebrates Canadian literature by commemorating the locations in which stories and poems are set, for the first bookmark in Prince Edward Island, with an unveiling at the location of Montgomery's Cavendish home, where she was raised by her maternal grandparents, on 24 June 2018.

PRELUDE

"The Poet's Thought" appeared in *The Canadian Magazine* of Toronto in April 1909; a clipping of this publication is in Scrapbook 8. Montgomery also included this poem in *The Watchman and Other Poems*. "Lucent" refers to something that is "shining, bright, luminous," according to the *OED*.

SONGS OF PLACE

"In Lovers' Lane" appeared in *The Delineator*, a prominent New York periodical, in July 1903; a clipping of this publication is in Scrapbook 6. It was subsequently published in *Poems*, in *The Watchman and Other Poems*, and in the May 1940 issue of *The Maritime Advocate and Busy East*, published in Sackville, New Brunswick. Harebells are wild hyacinths.

"The Fir Lane" appeared in the December 1904 issue of *Vick's Family Magazine* of Rochester, New York, and subsequently in the 6 September 1916 issue of *Zion's Herald*, a progressive Methodist weekly based in Boston, and the 10 November 1916 issue of the *Springfield Republican* of Massachusetts; clippings of the first two publications are in Scrapbook 8.

"In an Old Garden" appeared in the September 1907 issue of *The Canadian Magazine*; a clipping of this publication is in Scrapbook 8.

"The Old Home Calls" appeared in the 1 April 1909 issue of *The Youth's Companion*, a prominent Boston magazine for children; a clipping of this publication is in Scrapbook 8. It was subsequently published in *Woman's Century*, a Toronto periodical, in its June 1921 issue; a clipping of that publication is in Scrapbook 5. It also appeared in *The Watchman and Other Poems* as well as in *Canadian Poets*, chosen and edited by John W. Garvin, published by McClelland, Goodchild, and Stewart in 1916; a revised edition was published in 1926. (Garvin's volume was republished in 1916 by

Frederick A. Stokes Company as *Canadian Poets and Poetry*.) The second stanza was excerpted in a posthumous tribute to Montgomery appearing in *Saturday Night* magazine in May 1942 along with her final poem, "The Piper" (see "[L.M. Montgomery's Last Poem]").

"The Exile" appeared in the 22 January 1913 issue of *Zion's Herald* and in the 9 February 1913 issue of the *Springfield Republican*; a clipping of the first publication is in Scrapbook 8.

"The Summons" appeared in the 16 March 1914 issue of *The Sabbath Recorder*, published in Plainfield, New Jersey. An unidentified and undated clipping of another published version of this poem is in Scrapbook 8.

SONGS OF MEMORY

"Three Days" appeared in the September 1901 issue of *National Magazine*, then published jointly in Boston and Buffalo; a clipping of this publication is in Scrapbook 1.

"Companioned" appeared in the August 1910 issue of *The Canadian Magazine*; a clipping of this publication is in Scrapbook 8. In this context, the word "orient" refers to daybreak.

"Do You Remember?" appeared in the January 1911 issue of *The Canadian Magazine*; a clipping of this publication is in Scrapbook 8.

"Memory Pictures" appeared in the September 1912 issue of *The Canadian Magazine*; a clipping of this publication is in Scrapbook 8. "Pleasaunces" is an obsolete spelling of "pleasances." The Mary-lily (*Lilium candidum*) is also known as the Madonna-lily.

INTERLUDE

"The Singer" appeared in the 27 January 1906 issue of *The Ram's Horn*, a religious periodical located in Chicago; a clipping of this publication is in Scrapbook 8. In the original publication, part of the last line of the first stanza reads as "grave years and youth"; in her scrapbook copy, Montgomery corrects this in ink to read "gray years and golden youth."

SONGS OF LAMENTATION

"Irrevocable" appeared in the 10 November 1898 issue of *The Congregationalist*, a Boston paper; a clipping of this publication is in Scrapbook 2. "Upas" is an archaic word referring to "a baleful, destructive, or deadly power or influence," according to the *OED*.

"I Would Be Well" appeared in the 7 March 1900 issue of the *Portland Transcript*,(Maine), a weekly paper; a clipping of this publication is in Scrapbook 2.

"Night Watches" appeared in the 28 July 1900 issue of *The New York Family Story Paper*; a clipping of this publication is in Scrapbook 2. "Grewsome" is an archaic spelling of "gruesome."

"If I Had Known" appeared in the 18 February 1903 issue of *Zion's Herald*; a clipping of this publication is in Scrapbook 6.

"The Book" appeared in the January 1906 issue of *The Designer*, a New York magazine; a clipping of this publication is in Scrapbook 8.

"Longing" appeared in the May 1907 issue of *Donahoe's Magazine*, a Catholic periodical based in Boston, and with slight changes in the 8 September 1915 issue of *Zion's Herald*; clippings of both publications are in Scrapbook 8.

"The Mother" appeared in *The Watchman and Other Poems*. In November 1916, when that book was published, Montgomery's two surviving sons were four years and thirteen months old, respectively.

SONGS OF WAR

"The Last Prayer," signed Lucy Maud Montgomery, appeared in *The College Record*, the short-lived student paper of Prince of Wales College, sometime toward the end of the 1893–1894 school year, during which Montgomery undertook her teacher training; Montgomery's handwritten note accompanying the clipping of this poem in Scrapbook 7 indicates that it was published in the March 1894 issue, but it does not appear in either the March or the April issues of the magazine, which are the only issues I have been able to locate.

"Albion" refers to the earliest known name of the island of Great Britain, suggesting a British soldier.

"The Three Songs" appeared in the March 1908 issue of *The New Age*, a magazine published out of Washington, DC; a clipping of this publication is in Scrapbook 8. "Doughty" is an archaic word referring to something heroic or virtuous.

"We Who Wait" appeared in the 12 August 1914 issue of *Zion's Herald*, merely a week after England declared war on Germany; a clipping of this publication is in Scrapbook 8. "Guerdoned" is an archaic word meaning "rewarded."

"Our Women" appeared in *Canadian Poems of the Great War*, edited by John W. Garvin and published by McClelland and Stewart in 1918. It was subsequently republished in the following books: *Songs of the Maritimes: An Anthology of the Poetry of the Maritime Provinces of Canada*, edited by Eliza Ritchie and published by McClelland and Stewart in 1931, under the title "Our Women (Written in War-Time)"; *We Stand on Guard: Poems and Songs of Canadians in Battle*, compiled by John Robert Colombo and Michael Richardson and self-published in 1985; and a restored and annotated edition of L.M. Montgomery's novel *Rilla of Ingleside*, edited by Benjamin Lefebvre and Andrea McKenzie and published by Viking Canada in 2010.

INTERLUDE

"One of the Shepherds" appeared in the 24 December 1908 issue of *The Christian Endeavor World*, an interdenominational Protestant magazine located in Boston; a clipping of this publication is in Scrapbook 8. It also appears in *The Watchman and Other Poems*. It subsequently was reprinted, unsigned, in the 20 December 1919 issue of *The Canadian Countryman*, a Toronto periodical. "Khan" is an Arabic word meaning "inn."

SONGS OF LAND AND SEA

"When the Fishing Boats Go Out" appeared in the 14 September 1899 issue of *The Youth's Companion*; a clipping of this publication is in Scrapbook 2. Montgomery also included it in *Poems* and in *The Watchman and Other Poems*.

"When the Fishing Boats Come In" is believed to have appeared in the January 1899 issue of *The Weekly Bouquet*, a Boston magazine; a clipping with these bibliographical details is in Scrapbook 2. It later appeared in the 1 October 1910 issue of *East and West: A Paper for Young Canadians*, published in Toronto; a clipping of this version is in Scrapbook 8.

"Rain in the Woods," signed Lucy M. Montgomery, appeared in the August 1899 issue of *Sports Afield*, a Chicago magazine; a clipping of this publication is in Scrapbook 2.

"My Pictures" appeared in the May 1906 issue of *The Farm Journal* of Philadelphia; a clipping of this publication is in Scrapbook 8.

"The Wind in the Poplars" appeared in the October 1906 issue of *Sports Afield*; a clipping of this publication is in Scrapbook 8. "Threnody" refers to "a song of lamentation," such as "a lament for the dead," according to the *OED*.

"The Sea-Shell" appeared in the *Evening Times* of Grand Forks, North Dakota, on 20 January 1909. An unidentified clipping of another, identical version of this poem is in Scrapbook 8. The line "A merry lilt o' moonlight for mermaiden revelry!" is quoted by a supporting character as being a line from a poem by Walter Blythe in *Rilla of Ingleside* (see *RI*, 42).

"Before Storm" appeared in the November 1909 issue of *The Canadian Magazine*; a clipping of this publication is in Scrapbook 8. Montgomery subsequently included it in *The Watchman and Other Poems*. "Dolour" is an obsolete word referring to pain or physical suffering.

"A Shore Picture" appeared in the April 1910 issue of *The Canadian Magazine*; a clipping of that publication is in Scrapbook 8. The *OED* defines "argosy" as "a merchant-vessel of the largest size and burden" and a pennon as "a long narrow triangular or swallow-tailed flag, usually attached to the head of a lance or a helmet."

"The Sea to the Shore" appeared in *The Watchman and Other Poems*.

SONGS OF DEATH

"Too Late" appeared in the 31 August 1901 issue of *The Ram's Horn*; a clipping of this publication is in Scrapbook 6.

"I Have Buried My Dead" appeared in the 12 October 1901 issue of *The New York Family Story Paper*; a clipping of this publication is in Scrapbook 1.

"Omega" appeared in the 31 January 1903 issue of *Waverley Magazine*, a Boston periodical; a clipping of this publication is in Scrapbook 6.

"An Old Man's Grave" appeared in the 6 December 1906 issue of *The Youth's Companion*; a clipping of this publication is in Scrapbook 8. It also appeared, under the title "The Old Man's Grave," in *The Watchman and Other Poems*, in two editions of Garvin's *Canadian Poets*, and in chapter 22 of *Anne of Ingleside* (see *AIn*, 144). "Meet" in this context refers to something "suitable, fit, proper for some purpose or occasion, expressed or implied," according to the *OED*.

"The Treasures" appeared in the 30 May 1907 issue of *The Christian Endeavor World*; a clipping of this publication is in Scrapbook 8.

SONGS OF LOVE

"If Love Should Come" appeared in *Munsey's Magazine* of New York in December 1897; a clipping of this publication is in Scrapbook 2. Although "aye" is still used under some circumstances as a way to vote "yes" on a motion, here Montgomery uses it in the sense of "evermore."

"Assurance" appeared in the 10 March 1900 issue of *The New York Family Story Paper*.

"The Gray Silk Gown," signed Joyce Cavendish, appeared in the 23 May 1903 issue of *The New York Family Story Paper*; a clipping of this publication is in Scrapbook 6.

"On the Bridge," signed Joyce Cavendish, appeared in the 11 June 1904 issue of *The New York Family Story Paper*; a clipping of this publication is in Scrapbook 3.

"Gratitude" appears in an unidentified and undated clipping in Scrapbook 8. It also appears in the *Walnut Valley Times* of El Dorado, Kansas, on 9 March 1907 and again on 15 March of that year.

"With Tears They Buried You To-day" appeared in *The Canadian Magazine* in September 1914; a clipping of this publication is in Scrapbook 5. It also appeared in *The Watchman and Other Poems*.

"Forever" appeared in *The Watchman and Other Poems*. An earlier and shorter version, with minor variants and ending with the line "And on harvest noons," appeared in *The Canadian Magazine* in August 1916.

"To One Hated" appeared in *The Watchman and Other Poems*. The proverb "Hate is only Love that has missed its way" appears again in Montgomery's novels *A Tangled Web* (see TW, 117) and *Anne of Windy Poplars* (see AWP, 60).

"The Lover's Catechism" appeared in the March 1921 issue of *Breezy Stories*, a New York magazine.

POSTLUDE

"The Poet" appeared in *The Watchman and Other Poems*.

CODA

"What I Would Ask of Life" was published in *The American Messenger* in December 1912; a clipping of this publication is in Scrapbook 8.

Bibliography

Arizona Republican (Phoenix). "Two Songs of Love." 18 December 1898, 5.

"Author Tells How He Wrote His Story." In Lefebvre, *The L.M. Montgomery Reader*, 1: 33–34.

Bentley, D.M.R. "Post-Confederation Poetry." In *The Cambridge History of Canadian Literature*, edited by Coral Ann Howells and Eva-Marie Kröller, 127–43. Cambridge: Cambridge University Press, 2009.

Bode, Rita, and Lesley D. Clement, eds. *L.M. Montgomery's Rainbow Valleys: The Ontario Years, 1911–1942*. Montreal and Kingston: McGill-Queen's University Press, 2015.

Bode, Rita, and Jean Mitchell, eds. *L.M. Montgomery and the Matter of Nature(s)*. Montreal and Kingston: McGill-Queen's University Press, 2018.

Boone, Laurel. "Bliss Carman's Pageants, Masques and Essays and the Genesis of Modern Dance." In *Bliss Carman: A Reappraisal*, edited by Gerald Lynch, 165–80. Ottawa: University of Ottawa Press, 1990. Reappraisals: Canadian Writers 16.

Campbell, Wilfred, ed. *The Oxford Book of Canadian Verse*. 1913. Toronto: Oxford University Press, 2013.

Collins, Carolyn Strom. "L.M. Montgomery's 'Little Booklet of Verse.'" *The Shining Scroll* 2010, Part 3, 14–21.

Crawford, Isabella Valancy. *The Collected Poems of Isabella Valancy Crawford*. Edited by J.W. Garvin. Toronto: William Briggs, 1905.

Daniells, Roy. "Crawford, Carman, and D.C. Scott." In Klinck, *Literary History of Canada*, 422–37.

———. "Lampman and Roberts." In Klinck, *Literary History of Canada*, 405–21.

———. "Minor Poets 1880–1920." In Klinck, *Literary History of Canada*, 438–46.

Epperly, Elizabeth Rollins. *The Fragrance of Sweet-Grass: L.M. Montgomery's Heroines and the Pursuit of Romance*. 1992. Toronto: University of Toronto Press, 2014.

———. *Imagining Anne: The Island Scrapbooks of L.M. Montgomery*. Toronto: Penguin Canada, 2008. 100 Years of Anne.

Ferns, John. "'Rainbow Dreams': The Poetry of Lucy Maud Montgomery." *Canadian Children's Literature / Littérature canadienne pour la jeunesse* 42 (1986): 29–40.

Fisher, Susan. "'Watchman, What of the Night?' L.M. Montgomery's Poems of War." In McKenzie and Ledwell, *L.M. Montgomery and War*, 94–109.

Garvin, John W., ed. *Canadian Poems of the Great War*. Toronto: McClelland and Stewart, 1918.

———, ed. *Canadian Poets*. Toronto: McClelland, Goodchild, and Stewart, 1916. Also as *Canadian Poets and Poetry*. New York: Frederick A. Stokes Company, 1916.

———, ed. *Canadian Poets*. Toronto: McClelland and Stewart, 1926.

———, ed. *Canadian Verse for Boys and Girls*. Toronto: Thomas Nelson and Sons, 1931.

Gerson, Carole. "The Business of a Woman's Life: Money and Motive in the Careers of Early Canadian Women Writers." In *Women's Writing and the Literary Institution / L'Écriture au féminin et l'institution littéraire: Proceedings of a Conference*, edited by Claudine Potvin, Janice Williamson, and Steven Tötösy de Zepetnek, 77–94. Edmonton: Research Institute for Comparative Literature, University of Alberta, 1992.

Gerson, Carole, and Gwendolyn Davies, eds. *Canadian Poetry from the Beginnings through the First World War*. 1994. Toronto: McClelland and Stewart, 2010. New Canadian Library.

Groening, Laura. "The Poetry of Lucy Maud Montgomery." Review of *The Poetry of Lucy Maud Montgomery*, selected by John Ferns and Kevin McCabe. *The Atlantic Provinces Book Review* (Halifax), May–June 1988, 7.

Hale, Katherine. "About Canadian Writers: L.M. Montgomery, the Charming Author of 'Anne.'" In Lefebvre, *The L.M. Montgomery Reader*, 1: 241–43.

——. *Isabella Valancy Crawford*. Toronto: The Ryerson Press, n.d. [1923]. Makers of Canadian Literature.

Harrison, Dick. "Stead, Robert J.C." In Toye, *The Oxford Companion to Canadian Literature*, 771–72.

——. "Stringer, Arthur." In Toye, *The Oxford Companion to Canadian Literature*, 775.

Karr, Clarence. *Authors and Audiences: Popular Canadian Fiction in the Early Twentieth Century*. Montreal and Kingston: McGill-Queen's University Press, 2000.

Klinck, Carl F., ed. *Literary History of Canada: Canadian Literature in English*, Volume 1. 2nd ed. 1976. Toronto: University of Toronto Press, 1977.

Lefebvre, Benjamin. "Epilogue: Posthumous Titles, 1960–2013." In Lefebvre, *The L.M. Montgomery Reader*, 3: 351–90.

——. "Introduction: A Critical Heritage." In Lefebvre, *The L.M. Montgomery Reader*, 2: 3–49.

——. "Introduction: A Legacy in Review." In Lefebvre, *The L.M. Montgomery Reader*, 3: 3–48.

——. "Introduction: A Life in Print." In Lefebvre, *The L.M. Montgomery Reader*, 1: 3–28.

——, ed. *The L.M. Montgomery Reader*, Volume 1: *A Life in Print*; Volume 2: *A Critical Heritage*; Volume 3: *A Legacy in Review*. Toronto: University of Toronto Press, 2013, 2014, 2015.

"[L.M. Montgomery's Last Poem]." In Lefebvre, *The L.M. Montgomery Reader*, 1: 375–77.

McCabe, Kevin. "Budding Poetess." In *The Lucy Maud Montgomery Album*, compiled by Kevin McCabe, edited by Alexandra Heilbron, 146–51. Toronto: Fitzhenry and Whiteside, 1999.

——. Introduction to Montgomery, *The Poetry of Lucy Maud Montgomery*, 2–19.

——. "Lucy Maud Montgomery: The Person and the Poet." *Canadian Children's Literature / Littérature canadienne pour la jeunesse* 38 (1985): 68–80.

McKenzie, Andrea, and Jane Ledwell, eds. *L.M. Montgomery and War*. Montreal and Kingston: McGill-Queen's University Press, 2017.

Montgomery, L.M. *After Green Gables: L.M. Montgomery's Letters to Ephraim Weber, 1916–1941*. Edited by Hildi Froese Tiessen and Paul Gerard Tiessen. Toronto: University of Toronto Press, 2006.

——. *Anne of Green Gables*. Boston: L.C. Page and Company, 1908.

————. *Anne of Ingleside*. Toronto: McClelland and Stewart, 1939.

————. *Anne of the Island*. Boston: The Page Company, 1915.

————. *Anne of Windy Poplars*. Toronto: McClelland and Stewart, 1936.

————. *Anne's House of Dreams*. Toronto: McClelland, Goodchild, and Stewart, 1917.

————. "An Autobiographical Sketch." In Lefebvre, *The L.M. Montgomery Reader*, 1: 254–59.

————. "Blank Verse? 'Very Blank,' Says Father." In Lefebvre, *The L.M. Montgomery Reader*, 1: 180–81.

————. *The Blue Castle*. Toronto: McClelland and Stewart, 1926.

————. *The Blythes Are Quoted*. Edited by Benjamin Lefebvre. Toronto: Viking Canada, 2009.

————. "Book Price Record Book, 1908–1942." XZ1 MS A098043, L.M. Montgomery Collection, Archival and Special Collections, University of Guelph Library.

————. "The Bride Dreams." *The Canadian Bookman* (Toronto), March 1922, 101.

————. *The Complete Journals of L.M. Montgomery: The PEI Years, 1889–1900*. Edited by Mary Henley Rubio and Elizabeth Hillman Waterston. Toronto: Oxford University Press, 2012.

————. *The Complete Journals of L.M. Montgomery: The PEI Years, 1901–1911*. Edited by Mary Henley Rubio and Elizabeth Hillman Waterston. Toronto: Oxford University Press, 2013.

————. *Emily Climbs*. Toronto: McClelland and Stewart, 1925.

————. *Emily of New Moon*. Toronto: McClelland and Stewart, 1923.

————. *Emily's Quest*. Toronto: McClelland and Stewart, 1927.

————. *The Green Gables Letters from L.M. Montgomery to Ephraim Weber, 1905–1909*. Edited by Wilfrid Eggleston. Toronto: The Ryerson Press, 1960.

————. "How I Began." In Lefebvre, *The L.M. Montgomery Reader*, 1: 144–47.

————. "How I Began to Write." In Lefebvre, *The L.M. Montgomery Reader*, 1: 67–72.

————. *Kilmeny of the Orchard*. Boston: L.C. Page and Company, 1910.

————. *L.M. Montgomery's Complete Journals: The Ontario Years, 1911–1917*. Edited by Jen Rubio. N.p.: Rock's Mills Press, 2016.

————. *L.M. Montgomery's Complete Journals: The Ontario Years, 1918–1921*. Edited by Jen Rubio. N.p.: Rock's Mills Press, 2017.

————. *Mistress Pat: A Novel of Silver Bush*. Toronto: McClelland and Stewart, 1935.

————. *My Dear Mr. M: Letters to G.B. MacMillan from L.M. Montgomery*. Edited by Francis W.P. Bolger and Elizabeth R. Epperly. Toronto: McGraw-Hill Ryerson, 1980.

————. *A Name for Herself: Selected Writings, 1891–1917*. Edited by Benjamin Lefebvre. Toronto: University of Toronto Press, 2018. The L.M. Montgomery Library.

———— [Lucy Maud Montgomery]. "On Cape Le Force." *Daily Patriot* (Charlottetown), 26 November 1890, 1.

————. *[Poems]*. N.p.: n.p., [1903?].

————. *The Poetry of Lucy Maud Montgomery*. Selected by John Ferns and Kevin McCabe. Markham, ON: Fitzhenry and Whiteside, 1987.

————. *Rilla of Ingleside*. Toronto: McClelland and Stewart, 1921.

————. *The Road to Yesterday*. Toronto: McGraw-Hill Ryerson, 1974.

————, comp. Scrapbooks 1–12. PEI.OSZ PS 8525.068 A16 1981, University Archives and Special Collections, University of Prince Edward Island Library.

————. *The Selected Journals of L.M. Montgomery*, Volume 4: *1929–1935*. Edited by Mary Rubio and Elizabeth Waterston. Toronto: Oxford University Press, 1998.

————. *The Story Girl*. Boston: L.C. Page and Company, 1911.

————. *The Watchman and Other Poems*. Toronto: McClelland, Goodchild, and Stewart, 1916; New York: Frederick A. Stokes Company, 1917; London: Constable and Company, 1920.

Parker, George L. "Carman, Bliss." In Toye, *The Oxford Companion to Canadian Literature*, 102–4.

————. "Roberts, Sir Charles G.D." In Toye, *The Oxford Companion to Canadian Literature*, 708–10.

Pollock, Zailig. "Lampman, Archibald." In Toye, *The Oxford Companion to Canadian Literature*, 423–25.

Ross, Catherine. "Crawford, Isabella Valancy." In Toye, *The Oxford Companion to Canadian Literature*, 145–47.

Rubio, Mary Henley. *Lucy Maud Montgomery: The Gift of Wings*. N.p.: Doubleday Canada, 2008.

"[Such a Delightful Little Person]." In Lefebvre, *The L.M. Montgomery Reader*, 1: 31–32.

Toye, William, ed. *The Oxford Companion to Canadian Literature*. Toronto: Oxford University Press, 1983.

"*The Watchman and Other Poems.*" In Lefebvre, *The L.M. Montgomery Reader*, 3: 172–79.

Waterston, Elizabeth. "Reflection Piece – The Poetry of L.M. Montgomery." In *L.M. Montgomery and Canadian Culture*, edited by Irene Gammel and Elizabeth Epperly, 77–84. Toronto: University of Toronto Press, 1999.

Wicken, George. "Scott, Duncan Campbell." In Toye, *The Oxford Companion to Canadian Literature*, 740–42.

Wilmshurst, Rea. "L.M. Montgomery's Use of Quotations and Allusions in the 'Anne' Books." *Canadian Children's Literature / Littérature canadienne pour la jeunesse* 56 (1989): 15–45.

———. "Quotations and Allusions in L.M. Montgomery's Other Novels." Toronto: n.p., 1990.

Zichy, Francis. "Confederation Poets." In Toye, *The Oxford Companion to Canadian Literature*, 140.

Index by Title

Index by Date

Index by First Line